Tewkesbury 1471

The last Yorkist victory

Campaign • 131

Tewkesbury 1471

The last Yorkist victory

Christopher Gravett • Illustrated by Graham Turner

Series editor Lee Johnson • *Consultant editor* David G Chandler

First published in Great Britain in 2003 by Osprey Publishing,
Midland House, West Way, Botley, Oxford OX2 0PH, UK
44-02 23rd St, Suite 219, Long Island City, NY 11101, USA
Email: info@ospreypublishing.com

Transferred to digital print on demand 2010

First published 2003
5th impression 2009

Printed and bound by PrintOnDemand-Worldwide.com Peterborough, UK

A CIP catalogue record for this book is available from the British Library

ISBN: 978 1 84176 514 3

Editor: Lee Johnson
Design: The Black Spot
Index by David Worthington
Maps by The Map Studio
3D bird's-eye views by The Black Spot
Battlescene artwork by Graham Turner
Originated by The Electronic Page Company, Cwmbran, UK
Typeset in Helvetica Neue and ITC New Baskerville

Dedication
To Jane and Joanna, as always, for enduring my interests with a good grace

Acknowledgements
I am grateful to the staff at Barnet Museum for their kindness in discussing the battle with me, and allowing me to examine the
cannonballs in their collection. Graham Javes kindly showed me the evidence for the spur from Barnet, and shared his knowledge
of the battle. Thanks also to Paul Perrone for providing information on Monken Hadley Church. I am very grateful to the staff at
Tewkesbury Abbey for allowing me to photograph the sacristy door, and for their generous offers of help.

Artist's note
Readers may care to note that the original paintings from which the colour plates in this book were prepared are available for
private sale. All reproduction copyright whatsoever is retained by the Publishers. All enquiries should be addressed to:

Graham Turner
PO Box 568
Aylesbury
Bucks
HP17 8ZX
UK

The Publishers regret that they can enter into no correspondence upon this matter.

The Woodland Trust
Osprey Publishing is supporting the Woodland Trust, the UK's leading woodland conservation charity, by funding the
dedication of trees.

www.ospreypublishing.com

KEY TO MILITARY SYMBOLS

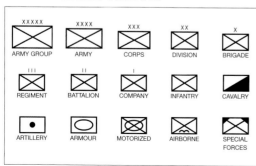

CONTENTS

ENGLAND IN 1471

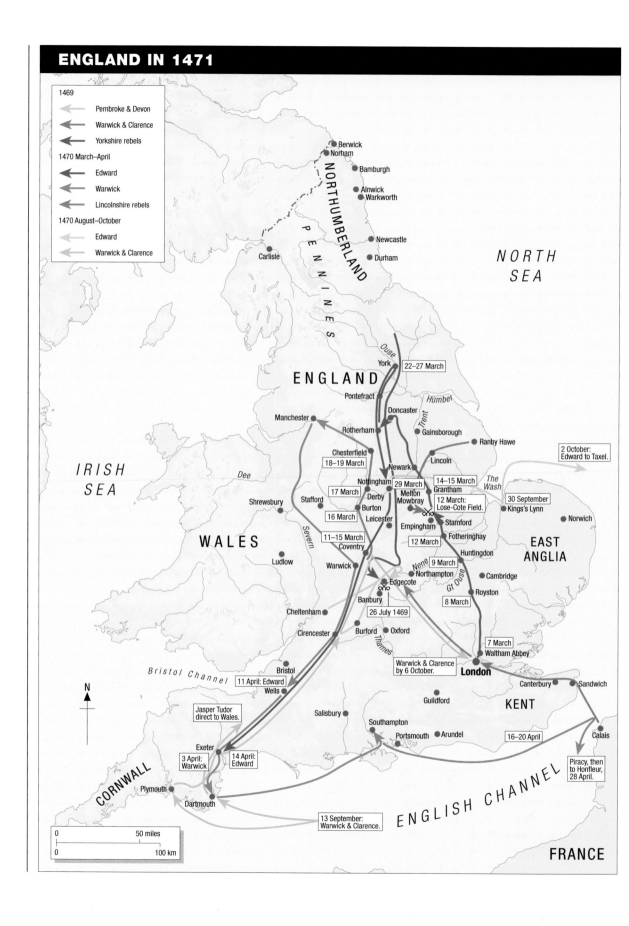

1469
- ⟶ Pembroke & Devon
- ⟶ Warwick & Clarence
- ⟶ Yorkshire rebels

1470 March–April
- ⟶ Edward
- ⟶ Warwick
- ⟶ Lincolnshire rebels

1470 August–October
- ⟶ Edward
- ⟶ Warwick & Clarence

NORTH SEA

IRISH SEA

ENGLAND

NORTHUMBERLAND

PENNINES

WALES

EAST ANGLIA

KENT

CORNWALL

Bristol Channel

ENGLISH CHANNEL

FRANCE

Berwick
Norham
Bamburgh
Alnwick
Warkworth
Newcastle
Durham
Carlisle
York · 22–27 March
Pontefract
Doncaster
Humber
Trent
Manchester
Rotherham
Gainsborough
Ranby Hawe
Chesterfield · 18–19 March
Lincoln
Newark
2 October: Edward to Taxel.
Nottingham · 29 March
Grantham · 14–15 March
The Wash
Shrewsbury
Stafford
17 March
Derby
Melton Mowbray
12 March: Lose-Cote Field.
30 September · King's Lynn
Norwich
Burton · 16 March
Leicester
Empingham
Stamford
EAST ANGLIA
11–15 March · Coventry
12 March
Fotheringhay
Ludlow
Warwick
Nene
9 March · Northampton
Huntingdon
Cambridge
Edgecote
Gt Ouse
Royston
Cheltenham
Banbury
8 March
Cirencester
26 July 1469
Burford · Oxford
Thames
7 March · Waltham Abbey
Bristol
Warwick & Clarence by 6 October.
11 April: Edward
Wells
London
Canterbury · Sandwich
Jasper Tudor direct to Wales.
Guildford
Salisbury
Southampton
Portsmouth · Arundel
16–20 April
Calais
Exeter · 3 April: Warwick · 14 April: Edward
Piracy, then to Honfleur, 28 April.
Plymouth
Dartmouth
13 September: Warwick & Clarence.

N

Dee
Severn

0 — 50 miles
0 — 100 km

INTRODUCTION

This book actually describes two battles that took place within a month of one another, Barnet and Tewkesbury. The same king, Edward IV, with his brother, Richard of Gloucester and his ally Lord Hastings, faced and defeated two separate Lancastrian forces to secure his throne. In the circumstances it seems logical to feature as one story Edward's entire campaign of 1471 to reassert his authority.

By the stirring events of April and May of 1471 the House of York would assert itself once more. It would entail the death of Edward's one-time friend and then rival, Richard Neville, Earl of Warwick, a lynchpin in the power politics of the day. It would see the execution of the young Duke of Somerset, another major figure, and, not least, the death in the Tower of the pitiful King Henry VI. The powerful and ambitious Queen Margaret of Anjou would see perhaps her final chance for the supremacy of the House of Lancaster shattered, as her royal husband, her new ally, Warwick, and her son were all killed. For Edward 1471 was a vital year for finally stamping his authority on his kingdom, leaving him free to carry out his foreign and domestic policies.

Genealogy of Edward IV. From illustrations in a 15th-century English work portraying Edward's early life, together with biblical scenes for religious emphasis. (By permission of the British Library, Ms Harley 7353)

Many details of the events of this period of 11 weeks come from the *History of the Arrivall of King Edward IV* (Stowe's Transcripts, British Library, Harleian 543). It appears to have been written by someone who was an eyewitness to much of what he wrote, which is implied in his note, but he refuses to give his name and refers to himself as 'an Anonymous'. He says he was a servant of Edward, and it is likely the man was a priest rather than a soldier, since nowhere does he suggest any involvement in the fighting that occurred, while he is careful to observe the royal religious devotions in high detail. Within days of Edward's return to London after Fauconberg's attacks, the *Short Arrivall* was written, and the *Arrivall* was produced within a year. The *Arrivall* was used by Holinshed in the 16th century, having been supplied by Fleetwood, Recorder of London, and is sometimes known as Fleetwood's Chronicle.

Also useful is Warkworth's Chronicle. This is a manuscript copy of Caxton's *Chronicle of the Brute*, with additions by Dr John Warkworth, Master of St Peter's College, Cambridge, from 1473 to 1500. Probably written in about 1479, the original is now lost but Warkworth had a duplicate, which survives. Together with these two important chronicles are

SIMPLIFIED GENEALOGICAL TREE
Showing the major royal family members involved in the Wars of the Roses

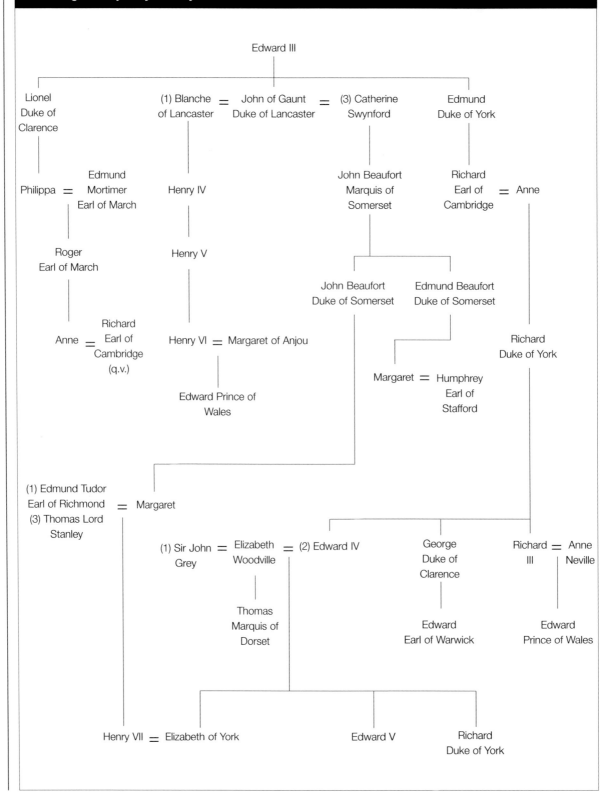

Portrait of Edward IV, painted in the early 16th century but based on a contemporary picture made before 1472. (By permission of the Royal Collection © Her Majesty the Queen)

the eyewitness accounts given in the Paston letters. Sir John Paston was present on the Lancastrian side at Barnet. The *Great Chronicle of London,* probably the work of Robert Fabian (died 1513), adds eyewitness accounts of events in the capital.

A small but noteworthy piece is the newsletter written by Gerhard von Wesel, a Hansa merchant writing home on events in London at the time of Barnet. Similarly the revolt in Lincolnshire in March 1470 is recorded in the *Chronicle of the Rebellion,* while *The Maner and Gwidynge* gives a propagandist account of events in July and August of that year at Angers.

Some foreign writers make mention of the events of 1471. Burgundy was for many years an ally of England. Both Philippe de Commines (*Mémoires*) and Jean de Waurin (*Recueil des Croniques et Anchiennes Histories de la Grant Bretaigne, à present nommé Engleterre*) were fairly unbiased and serious historians. Commines served Charles, Duke of Burgundy, and took part in the jousts to celebrate the latter's marriage to Edward's sister, Margaret of York. He later served Louis XI. Waurin served the Dukes, and had done some soldiering, having fought at Agincourt in 1415. He visited Warwick when he was in Calais in 1469.

The Tudor writers are variously biased towards the Lancastrian viewpoint, since Henry VII's parents were Lancastrians. Polydore Vergil came to England in 1502 and generally used his source material with care. Between about 1503 and 1513 he wrote his *Polydori Vergilii Urbinatis Anglicae Historiae Libri Vigintiseptem.* Though writing under the Tudor dynasty, he produced fairly unblemished accounts of earlier reigns. Hall translated Vergil in about 1540, adding material here and there, but not all can be verified. The Tudor writer Holinshed's *Chronicles of England, Scotland and Ireland* were actually produced by a syndicate, using the previous sources (especially the *Arrivall* and Hall) heavily to produce the version Shakespeare would employ.

Warwick's triumph

In April 1469 the north of England erupted into rebellion. The reasons for this are not totally clear. The first trouble appeared in April, when a leader calling himself Robin of Redesdale (or Robin Mend-All) gathered a force about him in Yorkshire. Redesdale was the territory of Sir John Conyers of Hornby in north Yorkshire, who was cousin by marriage to the Earl of Warwick. Though the rebels were broken up by John Neville, Earl of Northumberland, they came together again in Lancashire. With hardly a pause, a second revolt broke out in the East Riding of Yorkshire, this time under a leader using the name of Robin of Holderness (possibly a Robert Hillyard). The reason may have been resentment of the claim by St Leonard's Hospital in York to take 24 sheaves of corn from each ploughland, but this comes only from the account by Vergil who was not a contemporary. Once again, John Neville acted successfully in dispersing the rebels as they marched on York, Robin being beheaded. Some of the residue may have joined Redesdale and by the end of June his regrouped

**Portrait of Henry VI. A picture
painted in about 1515. (National
Portrait Gallery)**

force was moving south from Yorkshire and recruiting impressive numbers of followers. The attraction seems to have been a mixture of Neville influences and general disaffection with government. Warwick himself did little to attract suspicion, contenting himself largely with naval preparations against expected opposition following the break with the Hanseatic League the previous year.

At first Edward did little to quell the unrest in the north. He set off on pilgrimage to Bury St Edmunds and Walsingham in early June, but by 18 June resolved to do something about the threat. Whilst at Norwich he issued letters to the royal wardrobe for the supply of banners, standards and coat armour, 40 jackets of velvet and damask with roses, and 1,000 jackets in murray and blue, the livery colours of the House of York, together with other necessary materials for the field. Richard of Gloucester, Earl Rivers and Lord Scales were joined now by the Dukes of Norfolk and Suffolk, and Edward moved north to Fotheringhay Castle. Here he remained for about a week as more men and materials arrived, then marched again, reaching Stamford on 5 July. From here he moved to Grantham, then Nottingham. When he arrived in Newark he received news that seems to have made him realise that the situation was more dangerous than he had expected. Redesdale was said to lead a force three times the size of his own. Aware that his own army was not growing as fast as hoped, Edward acted swiftly. A demand was sent out on 10 July to Coventry demanding the 100 archers he had asked for five days earlier, with more if possible. He pulled back to Nottingham, hoping to be strengthened soon by the troops he had asked of William Herbert, Earl of Pembroke, and Humphrey Stafford, newly created Earl of Devon.

The situation was now becoming serious. Redesdale was coming closer and trying to outflank the royalist forces by marching south. To scotch any disputes over the disliked Woodvilles, Edward packed off Earl Rivers and his son to Wales, and Lord Scales to Norfolk. He wrote to his brother Clarence, to Warwick and the Archbishop of York, asking them to deny rumours of disloyalty. It was a lost cause. Warwick was adding the final touches to his designs to marry Clarence to his attractive daughter, Isabel, telling his men at Coventry the news, something of which Edward may have now heard. Warwick, Clarence and the Archbishop, joined on 4 July by John de Vere, Earl of Oxford, crossed from Sandwich to Calais, where the marriage took place. Edward could be in no doubt of the situation, for an open letter was now issued that stated their case, including demands for the removal of a number of Edward's favourites and indirect threats to Edward himself. Having called a muster at Canterbury for 16 July, Warwick and the others landed in Kent and moved up to the city. They left on about 18 July and arrived outside London, where they were admitted by the mayor, who had an eye to minimising damage and gave them a loan of £1,000. They then moved north towards Coventry, to link up with Redesdale, now being threatened by Pembroke and Devon.

Edward apparently did very little. No commissions of array were called, and he probably did not realise what little support either he or his government now enjoyed. He may have not wanted to believe that his own brother had turned on him, and Warwick was after all still using a smoke-screen of innocence. Edward seems to have left Pembroke and Devon to deal with the rising, but on 25 July they appear to have quarrelled about billeting in Banbury, which lay ahead of them, and as a result the two nobles split up. The Welsh contingents under Pembroke camped near Edgecote, some miles from those of the Earl of Devon. Early the following morning rebel forces attacked suddenly, Pembroke's men suffering particularly from a lack of archers, who were with Devon. Even when the latter appeared his men either never properly engaged or else arrived when it was too late. The accounts of the battle are quite confused and make a detailed analysis difficult. What may have finally turned the tide for the rebels were the troops under John Clapham, one of Warwick's supporters, whose arrival was mistaken for the vanguard of Warwick's own army. A number of rebel leaders had been slain but this could not prevent the defeat; Devon fled and Pembroke was captured along with his brother. Next day Warwick had them beheaded, not because they were traitors (which they were not, since they had not taken up arms against a king he supported) but because they had thwarted him in Wales and displaced him in royal favour.

On 29 July Edward left Nottingham and headed for Northampton, blissfully unaware of the disaster at Edgecote and expecting to join up with the Earls. On approaching the town he learned the awful truth and was promptly deserted by the majority of his men. He pressed on towards London with what remained of his force, but was confronted by Archbishop Neville and, with no chance of salvation, arrested. He was not harmed but shown courtesy, more than could be said for his relatives. While Edward was conveyed to Warwick Castle a prisoner, the hunt was on for the Woodvilles. On 12 August Sir John Woodville and Earl Rivers were executed outside Coventry, having been seized beyond the Severn. Sir Thomas Herbert was beheaded in Bristol, and the Earl of Devon captured by the people of Bridgwater and put to death on 17 August. The Earl of Warwick now seemed to hold all the cards.

However, he was soon to discover that all was not well. Few of the Earl's supporters benefited from the lands and offices that had fallen vacant, and the number of nobles who backed him was not high. Unrest followed; riots broke out in London, while nobles took the chance to settle old scores. The Duke of Norfolk besieged Caistor Castle that was held by the Paston family, the siege being described in their famous letters. Sir Humphrey Neville of Brancepeth and his brother, Charles, began a revolt on the northern borders in the name of Henry VI. Despite the lacklustre nature of this latter episode, Warwick tried raising troops against the Nevilles, but with little success. Unless Edward was released, Warwick would find meagre support. Now in Middleham, where Edward had been taken late in August, Warwick acquiesced and Edward was seen in York on 10 September. Together they raised troops, crushed the revolt and the Neville brothers were executed in York on 29 September.

Now Edward summoned Gloucester and the other members of his council and then rode south. By the middle of October, in full state, he was met on the London road by the mayor and representatives from the city. Established once more, Edward did little to alienate either his brother, Clarence, or Warwick. The latter, however, was not yet finished. Realising he could not use Edward for his own ends, he turned his attention to Clarence. Warwick failed to realise, or simply ignored, the fact made obvious from the past months, that the people were not keen to support anyone else, even though Clarence was Edward's own brother.

Portrait of Richard of Gloucester when Richard III, probably the earliest surviving picture of him, painted about 1515–22. (Society of Antiquaries of London)

Meanwhile events were to provide the opportunity for fomenting trouble. In the spring of 1470 a feud between Sir Thomas Burgh (Edward's master of the horse) and Richard, Lord Welles and Willoughby, resulted in the former being forced out of Lincolnshire. Edward came north to assert royal authority and restore order but, despite pardons for some of the nobles involved, his moves were seen as hostile. Men in Yorkshire and Lincolnshire suspected he would renege on recent royal pardons, and the latter found a leader in Lord Welles's son, Sir Robert. Hearing of this at Waltham Abbey in Essex on 7 March, Edward reached Royston next day, where news came to him of large numbers of rebels in Yorkshire and elsewhere, now heading for Stamford in Lincolnshire. Warwick sent to Edward assuring him that he and Clarence would join him, for Edward replied with letters authorising them to array troops in Warwickshire and Worcestershire. On 9 March Edward reached Huntingdon; here the prisoners Lord Welles and Sir Thomas Dymmock joined him, and Welles was forced to write to his son that he and Dymmock would be executed if he did not yield. Two days later Edward reached Fotheringhay, where he

learned that the enemy was marching towards Leicester where they were to meet another body under Warwick. Sir Robert, who was with Warwick, received his father's letter and refused to go on. On 12 March Edward arrived at Stamford and, on learning that the rebels were arrayed at Empingham, executed Welles and Dymmock and marched out against them. In the rout that followed so many rebel soldiers threw away their jackets that it became known as the battle of Lose-Cote Field. Rebel shouts of 'A Clarence! A Warwick!' during the battle, the wearing of Warwick's livery, and treasonable messages from the Duke and Earl found in an abandoned helmet, are said to have been the first proof Edward had of the others' duplicity. Whether Edward now doubted his brother's loyalty or not, he sent word to Clarence and Warwick to disband their commissioned men except for a decent number, but, despite assurances, they instead made for Burton-on-Trent. When Edward arrived at Grantham on 14 March the captured rebel leaders confessed that the whole revolt was largely down to Clarence and Warwick in order to usurp the throne for Clarence. In addition, revolts again broke out, this time in Richmondshire and the West Country, though the former trouble dissipated as news of Lose-Cote Field was heard. At Doncaster, Sir Robert Welles and Richard Warin were publicly executed on 19 March in front of the Yorkist troops. Edward's forces were now becoming formidably impressive. The Dukes of Norfolk and Suffolk and the Earl of Worcester had joined him when he marched from Doncaster on 20 March. Warwick was far weaker and could rely on little support now; his own brother, John Neville, Earl of Northumberland, stayed clear and actively opposed the Yorkshire revolt. Lord Stanley offered little incentive and may have been thwarted in any desires by the approach of Richard of Gloucester, who had moved up from

Wales to assist Edward. From York Edward, sent to Warwick and Clarence on 24 March, giving them four days to come before him, otherwise they were to be seen as traitors, with a price of £1,000 or £100 annually for their capture. In fact Edward had already advised his officers in Ireland and Calais that Clarence had been replaced. On 25 March he replaced the loyal Neville as Earl of Northumberland with Henry Percy, the previous earl's son and from a family whose name meant something in the north, and though Neville was handsomely compensated with, among other things, the title of Marquis of Montagu, he was not a happy man.

A day or two later Edward left York and came south, summoning men en route. On 29 March he reached Nottingham; on 11 April he appeared at Wells and four days later had arrived at Exeter. From Manchester, Warwick and Clarence had fled south and from Dartmouth took ship together with the Countess and her daughters. Warwick first sailed to Southampton in the hope of seizing at least his ship, the *Trinity*, docked there. As luck would have it, Earl Rivers was there with his vessels for refitting, and Warwick's ships were rebuffed. Disappointed, he crossed the Channel in order to land at Calais, where his comrade, Lord Wenlock, held command, but here they received a hostile reception and had to pull back to avoid the guns in the fortress, whose garrison was Yorkist. However, some ships came over to Warwick, under command of his relative, the Bastard of Fauconberg. Thus reinforced, Warwick attacked a Flemish convoy on 20 March off Calais. Having captured all the ships, he beat off attacks in a running fight along the coast with Lord Howard's fleet, which nevertheless recaptured some vessels. Warwick landed in the Seine estuary in early May.

His presence in France caused King Louis XI some concern, partly because Warwick's ships annoyed both Burgundy and Brittany with their attacks. There was also the obvious danger of a show of force by Edward's fleet, and moves by England and Burgundy began to look ominous. Warwick wanted reconciliation with Queen Margaret of Anjou, and money to support his return. A Lancastrian victory would thus be of assistance to Louis in removing the English threat and providing an ally against Burgundy. Despite this, Louis was keen to be rid of Warwick and of Clarence, whose presence was equally undesirable. He called Margaret to a meeting, but neither she nor Warwick was going to come to an easy arrangement. Eventually a marriage was hammered out between Margaret's son and Warwick's daughter, the betrothal taking place at Angers Cathedral on 25 July.

Edward tried to ensure he had the most effective defence measures in place. In June he had issued commissions of array to counties along the

Edward IV sits on his throne atop a Wheel of Fortune, a device for illustrating the fickle fortunes of life. He is flanked by the church and the army, including his brothers Gloucester and Clarence. (By permission of the British Library, Ms Harley 7353)

south coast and Welsh border, and travelled to Dover and Sandwich to inspect the fortifications, putting the Earl of Arundel in control of Dover and the Cinq Ports. Calais had been placed in the hands of Wenlock but as Edward increasingly came to suspect his loyalties he first brought in Rivers, then ousted Wenlock entirely, putting Lord Howard in charge as lieutenant. Edward was aware of the value of ships, probably learned from Warwick, and Howard was used to controlling the fleet; it was already at sea on patrol against Hansa vessels, and additional ships, brought by Earl Rivers from Sandwich and also Southampton, now bolstered the royal vessels. Even some of Warwick's ships from Southampton could now be turned against him, since their capture there by Rivers. Moreover, Warwick's attacks on the coasts of Burgundy pushed the Burgundians into sending their own fleet to assist Edward. As a result, the French coasts and the Channel were liable to see ships hostile to both the French crown and the Lancastrians, ships that sat outside ports and prevented ingress or egress. Even the attack by Hansa ships on the English coast, which drew off Edward's vessels, could not be exploited by Warwick without a favourable wind, despite the Burgundians leaving at the same time for a refit. It did, however, break the blockade for a while, until the ships reappeared to resume their watch. Only a storm finally swept a path clear for Warwick's fleet to proceed.

This careful planning is not recognised by some chroniclers. Burgundians blamed Edward for not listening to warnings about Warwick passed to him from the Duke (Commines). Instead, he appeared to them to do little but go hunting, and to be close to Warwick's brothers, Montagu, and the archbishop of York. He was accused by Chastellain of overconfidence in his own ability to rout Warwick, whom the king obviously thought to be a coward in battle.

Edward was certainly lenient to many rebels, with pardons for those who submitted before 7 May and no confiscations of land. Even the Earl of Worcester's delight in impaling those captured at the fight at Southampton was not to be taken as the norm in Edward's kingdom. Edward was happy to see the good in people, some of whom, such as Montagu, perhaps hid their real feelings very well.

While threatened from the south, another problem surfaced in the north. Towards the end of July pro-Neville risings occurred in the North Riding of Yorkshire and also around Carlisle. These do not seem to have been too serious, judging from the relatively modest number of pardons issued afterwards, but that is not how it was seen at the time. Northumberland had obviously not yet got the north under control, and Montagu was mute. Remembering the problems of letting northern disturbances spread unchecked as in 1469, Edward decided to act with speed as he had in 1470. Edward left London and headed north. He reached York on 14 August and then marched to Ripon, but the revolt had dissolved before him and he returned to York. He remained in the area for a while, sending a letter on 7 September to the men of Kent instructing them how to stop a landing, and hoping he would soon be back in London. In the middle of the month, the invasion happened. Warwick landed, not in Kent but in the West Country, and Edward was still in Yorkshire.

Yorkist and Burgundian ships had prevented part of Warwick's fleet and its French escort from leaving Honfleur, whilst other Burgundian vessels blockaded his other ships in La Hogue and Barfleur. This state of affairs lasted until early September, when a fierce storm forced the raising of the blockades and the invasion fleet could set out. Margaret refused to let her son go with it, resolved to stay in France until Warwick's forces had subdued most of England. Meanwhile Warwick, Clarence and the Earls of Oxford and Pembroke set sail from La Hogue on 9 September. Probably on 13 September they made land; *Warkworth's Chronicle* names Devon as the place of disembarkation, other contemporary chronicles place it in the West Country. Though a later writer, Polydore Vergil maintains that the landing place was Dartmouth.

Edward marched from York but never reached London. He halted near Nottingham (or possibly Derby) expecting reinforcements from Montagu. However, he then heard that the latter had suddenly changed sides and now supported Warwick. Meanwhile Warwick and Clarence had declared support for Henry VI immediately on their landing, and men soon began to pour in. The earl of Shrewsbury and Lord Stanley soon joined the Earls of Oxford and Pembroke under their banners. Swelling their ranks as they marched, the Lancastrian army now moved up towards Coventry. Risings also broke out in Kent in support, and Southwark was attacked together with other London suburbs. Edward probably realised he faced a major crisis; popular support was ebbing away in favour of Warwick, and Edward's current location in the north, never particularly friendly to him, weakened his position in the south. Moreover Warwick was not a merciful man. Despite the chroniclers' comments about lack of fighting men, Edward still had substantial forces with him under his brother, Gloucester, and Rivers, Hastings, Howard, Say, Worcester and others. But support in the country was no longer there. Towns and cities either sided with Warwick or refused to help Edward. Under the circumstances there was little else to do but flee. He rode across country to the Wash, almost getting himself drowned in the process, and reached King's Lynn, which lay under the control of Rivers. On 2 October he set sail from here and headed for the Low Countries. Out on the open sea a Hanseatic fleet spotted him and gave chase, only giving up when Edward's vessels reached the coast at Alkmaar. Edward was in such a plight that he had to pay the ship's master with a furred robe. Luckily, Lord Gruuthuse was lord of Holland and represented Duke Charles of Burgundy; he was also known to Edward, who was received now as a guest, together with his brother, Gloucester, and Lords Rivers, Hastings and Say.

The Readeption of Henry VI, as it was known, was carried out with only minimal violence. The Earl of Worcester, John Tiptoft, had earned such a reputation for sadistic cruelty that he in turn received no mercy and was executed on Tower Hill in front of a large vengeful audience. Most other Yorkist men of rank were treated with leniency, largely because their support was necessary for the government to function; only seven peers

'Portrait of Louis de Gruuthuse', from the Master of the Portraits of Princes. (Stedelijk Museum Brugge, Groeningemuseum, inv. nr. 0.GR1557.I)

The house of Louis de Gruuthuse in Bruges.

were not summoned to parliament. All this left Warwick and Clarence in a rather unsatisfactory position. Clarence was unsure of the future because Warwick was in league with Margaret, who obviously demanded that her son, Edward, was recognised as the heir to the throne. It is not surprising, therefore, that Edward IV spent his time in exile trying to lure Clarence back to his side. For his part Warwick realised that support for him was questionable. King Henry was generally liked by the populace. However, with few real rebels punished, there was not a great amount of land to reward Warwick's supporters for their efforts and he probably distrusted many of them. Warwick was also caught up in Louis XI's aggression towards Duke Charles of Burgundy. Because of this the latter, who at first had kept a distance from the exiled Edward, gradually changed his attitude. While keeping a public neutrality, he secretly gave Edward 50,000 florins towards his return to England and, as Commines notes, three or four Dutch ships were prepared at Veere on the island of Walcheren. As well as wooing Clarence, Edward wrote to other likely supporters in England, and to Duke Francis of Brittany. He promised the Hansa towns attractive rights after he was back in England, enough to convince them to supply him with 14 ships, which he could keep for a further 15 days after landing. In February 1471 an invasion fleet of modest size began to assemble at Flushing. Rivers was in Bruges to secure additional ships, and English merchants there also provided monetary loans. John Lyster and Stephen Driver, English captains, also sailed into Flushing. Edward left for his fleet on 19 February and on 2 March embarked on the *Antony*, which belonged to the Burgundian admiral, Henry, Lord of Veere. The wind was not favourable, but Edward stayed on board for the next nine days. On 11 March he set sail with 36 ships and perhaps 1,200 men, including Flemish handgunners.

CHRONOLOGY

1455

22 May First Battle of St Albans. Drawn contest between the Lancastrians and Yorkists.

1459

23 September Battle of Blore Heath. Salisbury holds off the Lancastrians.
12–13 October Rout of Ludford. Yorkists are defeated and Richard of York, Edward, Salisbury and Warwick escape abroad.

1460

26 June Yorkist leaders return from exile.
July Battle of Northampton. Henry VI is captured by Yorkists.
September Richard of York claims the crown in London.
30 December Battle of Wakefield. Richard of York and Earl of Rutland killed.

1461

1–3 February? Battle of Mortimer's Cross. Edward defeats the Welsh Lancastrians.
17 February Second Battle of St Albans. The Yorkists are defeated.
1 March Edward is proclaimed king.
28 March Battle of Ferrybridge.
29 March Battle of Towton.
28 June Edward crowned in Westminster Abbey.
9 September Edward arrives at Bristol.
30 September Pembroke Castle surrenders to Herbert.
16 October Jasper Tudor, the Duke of Exeter and Welsh Lancastrians defeated at Twt Hill near Caernarfon.

1464

25 April Montagu routs Lancastrians at Hedgeley Moor.
1 May Edward marries Elizabeth Woodville at Stony Stratford.
15 May Battle of Hexham. Montagu decisively routs the Lancastrians.

1469

April Robin of Redesdale's revolt.
Early June Edward on pilgrimage in Norfolk.
4 July Richard of Warwick takes Clarence to Calais to wed his daughter, Isabel.
5 July Edward reaches Stamford.
18 July Warwick and Clarence leave Canterbury and arrive outside London.
25 July Pembroke and Devon quarrel about billets and split up.
26 July Lancastrian rebels defeat Pembroke and Devon at Edgecote.
27 July Pembroke and his brother are beheaded on Warwick's orders.
29 July Edward leaves Nottingham for Northampton. Hears of the disaster at Edgecote and the bulk of his men desert. Edward presses on towards London but is arrested by Archbishop Neville.
10 September Edward seen in York.
Mid-October Edward met by the mayor of London and reinstated.

1470

Spring Feud between Sir Thomas Burgh and Richard, Lord Welles and Willoughby, draws Edward north.

7 March Edward at Waltham Abbey in Essex, where he learns of the revolt.

8 March Edward reaches Royston.

9 March Edward reaches Huntingdon.

11 March Edward reaches Fotheringhay; he learns the enemy is marching towards Leicester.

12 March Edward arrives at Stamford. The rebels are arrayed at Empingham. Lord Welles and Sir Thomas Dymmock executed. Battle of Lose-Cote Field; rebels flee.

20 March Edward marches from Doncaster to York. Warwick's fleet attack a Flemish convoy off Calais.

24 March Edward gives Warwick and Clarence four days to submit.

26 or 27 March Edward leaves York.

29 March Edward reaches Nottingham.

11 April Edward reaches Wells.

15 April Edward reaches Exeter.

Early May Warwick arrives in Seine estuary.

25 July Betrothal of Warwick's daughter to Margaret's son at Angers Cathedral.

End of July Pro-Neville risings in the North Riding of Yorkshire and around Carlisle.

14 August Edward reaches York.

9 September Warwick, Clarence and the Earls of Oxford and Pembroke sail from La Hogue.

13 September? Warwick makes land, possibly in Devon, perhaps Dartmouth.

2 October Edward sails from Kings Lynn for Holland.

1471

February Invasion fleet assembles at Flushing.

19 February Edward leaves for his fleet.

2 March Edward embarks on the *Antony*.

11 March Edward's fleet sets sail for England.

14 March Edward lands at Ravenspur.

18 March Edward arrives in York.

20 March Edward leaves York for Nottingham.

2 April Edward at Warwick learns that Clarence is marching to his aid from Burford.

3 April Edward, Clarence and Gloucester reunited.

5 April The brothers leave Coventry.

10 April The brothers reach St Albans.

11 April The brothers enter London.

12 April Men arrive to swell Edward's army. Richard of Warwick reaches St Albans.

13 April Edward, Clarence and Gloucester march from London.

14 April BATTLE OF BARNET. Edward defeats and kills Warwick. Margaret lands at Weymouth.

15 April Edward returns to London. Henry VI is returned to the Tower.

19 April Edwards sets up headquarters at Windsor.

30 April Margaret at Bath. Edward leaves Windsor for Cirencester.

1 May Margaret arrives at Bristol. Edward arrives at Malmesbury.

2 May Margaret arrives at Berkeley. Edward arrives at Sodbury Hill.

3 May Margaret leaves Berkeley for Gloucester. Rebuffed, she marches to Tewkesbury. Edward leaves Sodbury, marches to Cheltenham and thence to Tredington.

4 May BATTLE OF TEWKESBURY

7 May Edward marches from Tewkesbury.

12 May Fauconberg's forces demand entry into London, but are beaten off.

13 May Rebel attack at Kingston rebuffed

14 May Second assault on London beaten off and rebels routed.

21 May Edward arrives in London. Henry VI murdered in the Tower.

1483

Edward IV dies. Accession of Edward V

Edward V never crowned. Accession of Richard III

OPPOSING COMMANDERS

YORKISTS

Visually **King Edward IV** was the ideal medieval commander. He was tall: when his coffin was opened in 1789 his skeleton measured 6ft 3¹/₂ inches. He was considered handsome: though the portraits show a slightly babyish and somewhat pudgy face, he had no trouble attracting female company, something of which he took full advantage. Born at Rouen in April 1442 and known as 'The Rose of Rouen', he was now almost 29 years old and appeared an affable, approachable leader who consulted with his subordinates and referred to his cavalry as 'my children'. When angry, however, he could be frightening, and also quite ruthless. After the battle of Mortimer's Cross in 1461 he had ten men of rank executed at Hereford; he ordered the Duke of Somerset executed after the Duke had taken sanctuary in the Abbey after the battle of Tewkesbury, though whether sanctuary extended to the Abbey is debated. Edward was the man ultimately responsible for the death of the simple Henry VI while a prisoner in the Tower in 1471 (although this was later blamed on Richard of Gloucester), and also for the execution there of his own brother, Clarence, though it must be admitted the King had been more than tolerant of the Duke's petulant nature and treachery. Despite this ruthless streak he was sometimes over-trusting and subsequently tricked by schemers such as Somerset.

Sandal Castle, where Edward arrived in March 1471 on his way to London. It was close to the site of his father's death in battle against Somerset.

The garter stall plate of John Neville, Marquis of Montagu, in St George's Chapel, Windsor. The two entwined annulets (rings) differenced his arms from those of his brother, the Earl of Warwick. (Reproduced by permission of the Dean and Canons of Windsor)

Edward was skilled in warfare and there is no doubt that he was physically brave. He was at the forefront of his troops at the battle of Towton in 1461, and would be again at Barnet and Tewkesbury ten years later. He could act swiftly when faced with a crisis. Thus he swung round to face and destroy the allied Lancastrian/Welsh rising at Mortimer's Cross, to crush it before it got out of hand. His speed gave him the victory at Lose-Cote Field near Empingham in 1470, when he defeated Sir Robert Welles before Warwick could join forces with him. In 1471 he wasted no time in marching to confront Warwick when he learned the earl was heading straight towards him in London, resulting in Edward's victory at Barnet. His decisive movements after his landing at Ravenspur in 1471 allowed him to avoid the enemy until he could gather his forces around him, and contrasts well with the dithering of the opposition. Yet Edward too could appear uncertain. On several occasions he did relatively little when faced with insurrections, particularly in the north. After Towton, for example, he missed the opportunity to make a show of force in the area, and left Montagu and Neville to keep a check on things. At other times he seemed unwilling to march, preferring to stay put, often at Fotheringhay, or moved slowly until, more often than not, the revolt was snuffed out by someone else or simply dissipated. This tendency to lethargy went with a love of the good life, which resulted in Edward becoming rather overweight and was probably the cause of his death in 1483 from a stroke.

Richard, Duke of Gloucester was physically the opposite of his elder brother, being small and slender, taking rather after his father in looks. However, he proved a loyal commander and never displayed any hint of betrayal, unlike Clarence. It has been suggested that this was partly because he feared Edward. Like his brother, Richard was a capable commander and physically brave. Both at Barnet and Tewkesbury he was in command of a battle, on the right at Barnet and left at Tewkesbury. Both times he acquitted himself well, though it is debatable whether his performance could be classed as brilliant, as has been suggested. Considering that his division overlapped the Lancastrian left at Barnet, Richard was unable to break up his opponent, unlike the Lancastrian Oxford at the other end, who also overlapped the enemy and routed them. His service in Scotland, hailed by contemporaries as the work of a military mind, was not outstanding, when placed under a modern spotlight.

Lord Hastings did not fare well at Barnet, partly no doubt because his men found their flank overlapped, but he was unable to do anything to rally them once they had broken. It is noteworthy that at Tewkesbury Edward appears to have reversed the layout of his army, placing Hastings on the right this time, probably because he would otherwise face the Duke of Somerset. Edward presumably thought his brother, Richard, would be better fitted to this task.

Little is known of the military ability of **George, Duke of Clarence**. He was certainly aggressive and wholly untrustworthy, fighting first for Warwick and then against him at Tewkesbury.

LANCASTRIANS

Richard, Earl of Warwick was a key player in the history of the time. Nicknamed 'the Kingmaker', a title whose accuracy has since been questioned, he was nevertheless an astute political mind, and it was here that his true genius lay. As a military commander, however, he was not of the first rank. He was by nature defensive, and lacked the assertiveness and military mind of either Edward or Gloucester. His use of a varied array of defensive tricks at the Second Battle of St Albans shows imagination, but the fact that he was still unable to think flexibly to throw back the Lancastrian attacks highlights his perhaps dubious qualities of leadership in the field. He did not possess the natural courage displayed by the royal brothers when faced with danger, despite Victorian attempts to portray him as the archetypal knight in shining armour. During the surprise attack on the Yorkists at Ferrybridge prior to the battle of Towton, his actions might be interpreted as approaching panic, and contrasts with Edward's decisive move to confront the problem. His refusal to come out of Coventry or to co-ordinate a three-pronged attack on Edward during the crucial phase after the Yorkist landings in 1471 again shows a lack of both physical courage and forward planning. At Barnet the only move the chroniclers comment upon is when he mounts his horse to flee when the battle turns against the Lancastrians; he dies ignominiously at the hands of ordinary unnamed soldiers. Despite his military record, he showed little sympathy for his captured enemies, and his cold-blooded execution in 1469 of Pembroke and his brother, Sir Richard, for no reason other than they were gaining over him in royal favour, shows the Earl's true colours. His lust for power is perhaps best seen in the way he was prepared to abase himself before his bitter enemy, Queen Margaret, and agree to the union of their children.

Warwick's brother, **John Neville, Marquis of Montagu**, was in the central battle at Barnet, and as Somerset was not present it is almost certain Montagu commanded it. Unlike Warwick, he was less obsessed with power. Despite approaches from his brother, he remained loyal to Edward for many years until he finally went over to the Lancastrian cause. He proved an astute soldier. After Towton in 1461, it was Montagu who largely looked after the north, obviously trusted to do so by Edward, who was often reluctant to come north himself. He showed himself a skilled tactician. In early June he routed a force that descended on Carlisle. In 1463, together with

The falcon and fetterlock badge of Edward IV, and the boar badge of Richard of Gloucester, from Fenn's book of badges, a collection of badges drawn between about 1466 and 1470 and later cut out and pasted into a book. (By permission of the British Library, (Ms Add. 40742, f.5)

21

Warwick and the Archbishop of York, he dispersed a rebel force attacking Norham. In April 1464 Montagu was sent north to escort the Scottish ambassadors. Managing to evade an ambush near Newcastle, he was then attacked around 25 April at Hedgeley Moor, nine miles from Alnwick, but routed the Lancastrians, met the Scots and escorted them to York. On 15 May 1464 Montagu marched 20 miles from Newcastle and fell on the rebel camp near Hexham. Almost all the leading nobles were killed or captured soon afterwards. Quite why Montagu allowed Edward to slip past him in 1471 is uncertain, and Warwick suspected his loyalty, which seems groundless.

Edmund Beaufort, Duke of Somerset was in charge of the Lancastrian army at Tewkesbury and was in direct control of the left battle. It is unlikely he took part at Barnet, since some chroniclers describe how he rode off to the West Country to await Queen Margaret. His fierce temper is illustrated in the remarkable, if questionable, killing of Lord Wenlock in what amounts to a summary execution for treason. However, his skill as a strategist can be seen in his feints to confuse Edward after Margaret had landed. His first false trail was not taken, but his second attempt, pretending to take up position at Sodbury, brilliantly caught out Edward and won precious time for the Lancastrians trying to reach the river crossings before the Yorkists.

John de Vere, Earl of Oxford was a respected military commander. His skills and the esteem he earned were evidenced at Barnet by the way he not only rallied about 800 of his troops during their pursuit of the enemy, but also that he managed to drag a large number of them from their looting in the town.

Commander of the left battle at Barnet, **Henry Holland, Duke of Exeter** was seriously wounded and narrowly avoided death. As his line was over-lapped by the Yorkist division under Gloucester, he appears to have held his ground until after the Hastings debacle and pursuit of Oxford on the other wing.

John, Lord Wenlock, Earl of Dorset had fought on the winning side at the Second Battle of St Albans (Lancastrian) and at Towton (Yorkist), which does not necessarily prove any great inherent military skill. His luck was to run out at Tewkesbury, when he had changed sides yet again. Not a man to chance his arm, he did nothing when Somerset's division ran into trouble and simply refused to come down and possibly turn the chaos into victory.

John Courtenay, Earl of Devon waited in the West Country for Queen Margaret to land, and commanded the left battle at Tewkesbury. He does not seem to have been an exceptional commander, and Edward probably rated him well below Somerset when he placed Lord Hastings opposite him before the battle.

OPPOSING ARMIES

The Yorkist and Lancastrian armies that took part in the campaign of 1471 were both essentially composed of men raised by the same systems and wearing similar equipment. The king (or queen) could call on great lords who themselves could field large numbers of men. Many of these were retainers, men who were contracted to serve a lord. As such, their terms of service were written down on parchment and a copy made below it, divided from the first by a wavy or indented line. The contract was then cut along this line and one half kept by the retainer and one by his lord. This indenture could then be verified in case of dispute by matching the two halves together. Retained men might live with their lord in his household. Called 'feed men', they performed everyday duties such as carrying messages, escort duty or conveying prisoners. In time of war they could prove most useful as they were on hand and ready for immediate action. Some retainers were given portions of land to live on; others (extraordinary retainers) held land some distance away, and had to travel to the rendezvous when summoned. 'Well willers' agreed to serve several lords, which was more profitable, but clauses had to be inserted in their contracts if they wished to avoid the difficulty of two masters summoning them to serve against each other. The retainers of great lords might well be knights or squires themselves. Squire at this date was a rank below knight and did not necessarily denote a youth in training, simply a man of knightly background who had not taken on the onerous duties of the knight, such as attendance at shire courts or even parliament. Other retainers, especially those who followed a lesser lord, might be squires or

Pontefract Castle was held by the Marquis of Montagu, whom Edward feared might attack as he passed. In the event, Montagu held off.

23

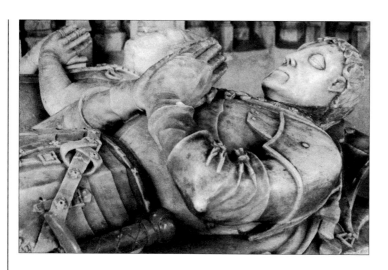

The effigy of the second Lord Saye and Sele, killed at Barnet, in Broughton Church, Oxfordshire. he wears a west European armour, the couters laced on at the elbows. Around his neck is a Yorkist collar of suns and stars. (By kind permission of Geoffrey Wheeler)

gentlemen, trained fighting men from non-noble families. Sometimes all those above the rank of yeomen were known as men-at-arms. The retainers of higher rank who answered a lord's summons might also bring retainers of their own, who served in the same way, but were instead archers or foot-soldiers, often billmen. This system of retaining men, known sometimes as bastard feudalism, meant that noblemen might be accompanied by large numbers of fighting men and cause trouble wherever they pleased, with scant regard for royal authority.

These retainers made up the professional core of a lord's force. They often wore jackets of the lord's livery, displaying the one or two main colours from his coat-of-arms. The jacket could often display a badge taken from an emblem of the lord's arms, similar to that which appeared on his standard – the long rallying flag that bore his colours and devices. Thus the system was sometimes called livery and maintenance. In order to augment this, however, the king or great lord might send out commissions of array, whereby a nobleman was detailed to find a set number of men for a designated period, with a certain amount of equipment. Towns were sometimes expected to send contingents but could be a law unto themselves, sending only a limited number or else backing the other side instead. Mercenary units included the Flemish handgunners procured by the Burgundians for Edward during his exile. The French contingent that accompanied Queen Margaret on her return to England in 1471 were presumably mercenaries who had agreed to join her and stay as long as they were paid but were possibly contracted troops serving for an agreed period.

Armies still tended to be organised into three traditional divisions or 'battles', the vanward, mainward and rearward, the van usually expected to hold the right of the line. A great nobleman or the monarch commanded each battle, and a smaller reserve might be employed at the rear if the divisions were placed in line. The knights, squires and men-at-arms largely fought on foot at this period, though knights and squires at least were trained to use a lance on horseback and all could wield hand weapons while mounted. However, cavalry was used selectively now, partly because of the increase in the use of mass archery, against which no horse was fully protected, and also the use of solid bodies of infantry with long staff weapons. Horsemen were still effective for scouting, skirmishing and surprise attacks. They might be placed on the wings of a division, or as a reserve where the 'prickers' could also discourage desertion. They were also very effective in chasing an enemy once his lines had broken. Dismounted knights might then call up their horses to do just that. However, men-at-arms now fought in fairly tight bodies, each lord surrounded by his retainers, his standard marking the rallying point and his banner, decorated with his personal coat-of-arms, identifying his own position. The soldiers of the commissions of array might also be organised in large bodies as part of each division.

Armour

The armour worn by the knights and squires at this date consisted of so-called 'alwite' harness, that is, armour made of plates that were not hidden under a riveted cloth covering. The standard of workmanship varied depending on the amount paid. The nobleman could demand the highest quality armour that covered him from head to foot – *cap-à-pie* armour. For the most part a western European style was in use in England, rather Italian in general form, but with some features more favoured in Germany. The enclosing visored Italian helmet called an *armet* was replaced by a visored *sallet* with or without a chin and throat defence, the *bevor*. The *placart* over the stomach was usually secured to the breastplate by a rivet in the German style, rather than a strap. The arm defences were often made in three separate parts instead of all being connected together, the sign of this being laces tied externally through the *couter* (elbow defence). Unlike the much larger Italian form of arm defence, English ones were usually symmetrical. The flutes that were becoming popular in Germany were also seen to some extent on west European armour. Already some tassets were being attached half way up the skirt, or *fauld*, rather than at the lower end. Gauntlets too showed a different construction than Italian ones. Some knights bought Italian armour, but even some of this might look English, since the north Italian armourers had a thriving trade in export armour made in the style of its destination. German armour seems to have been less popular. Flemish armourers also provided harnesses for English soldiers, though how, if at all, this differed from English work is not yet clear. For those who could not afford to have armour made in the great centres of north Italy, Germany or Flanders, armour pieces were selected from merchant armourers 'off the peg' in England, and fine adjustments made for a good fit. Some instead had to protect their torso with a stout 'brigandine', a canvas jacket lined with small pieces of plate, whose rivet heads could be seen at the front. Expensive versions were faced with rich cloths and had silvered or gilt rivet heads to produce an attractive garment. The brigandine might be worn with plate limb defences, or for the less wealthy with mail sleeves. For a few men the mail coat was still worn, presumably over a padded 'jack'. The 'jack' was the cheapest defence, being a padded jacket made from numerous layers of linen cloth, or sometimes perhaps tow, wool, or other wadding, and quilted to keep it in place. It was a surprisingly effective soft armour. Some might be reinforced with horn or metal plates, or perhaps even chain links down the outside of the sleeve. Some men may not have worn anything but their doublet. The *sallet* favoured with West European armour was also worn with brigandines, mail or jacks. As well as this, a simple round-topped iron or steel cap was worn, sometimes low enough to allow cut-outs for the ears. Both helmets were favoured by archers, as there was no brim over the face to hinder a bowstring. The kettle hat, rather like a 20th-century 'tin hat', was an alternative type, but its wide brim was not ideal for archers.

A north Italian *sallet* of about 1440–50, made for export to north Europe. The holes around the base of the skull are for rivets securing an internal lining band. (By courtesy of the Trustees of the Armouries, IV.5)

Weapons

The main weapon of the knight was his sword. It still retained the mysticism it had possessed for centuries, and was symbolically laid on the altar the evening before the knighting ceremony to imbue it with religious significance and provide a cross in the form of the hilt and guard. However, many men below the rank of knight now carried swords. The main fighting sword (the 'arming sword') was quite pointed and provided with sharpened edges, the main aim being to pierce the mail guarding the joints at the armpit or elbow, groin or neck, since the plate armour provided a glancing surface to guide a point away. Similarly the edge of the blade was less effective against plate, but could still be used against less well armed opponents, or in the rout when running men threw away their helmets and left their heads exposed to a pursuing horseman's swing. Some swords were acutely pointed, with a central rib to stiffen the blade, which gave it a flattened diamond section. These were thrusting weapons and sometimes had a long hilt to allow a two-handed grip for a powerful lunge. Some weapons had long blades, the so-called 'bastard sword' or hand-and-a-half sword, and could deal heavy blows to pummel a man to the ground. The dagger was less common than the sword and many effigies of men in plate armour omit it altogether, though it was a handy adjunct to the equipment of those less heavily armoured. The usual form used for war was the 'rondel' dagger, whereby a flat disc replaced the cross-guard and another might replace the pommel. Another type was the 'ballock' dagger, so-called because the two swellings at the lower end of the grip mimicked male genitalia. These daggers were usually provided with blades of triangular section, strong, stiff and ideal for thrusting. Since many armoured men now fought largely on foot, and since plate armour was considered so effective that a shield was unnecessary, two-handed staff weapons could be carried. The most popular for men of rank was the pollaxe, from the word for a head: 'poll'. Two versions were available. One consisted of an axe-head backed by a hammer and topped by a spike, the other had a hammer backed by a quadrilateral beak, again with a top spike. The haft was about 6ft long and its foot was shod with a socket with a short spike. Thus it could be used to cut, concuss or stab, depending on how used. This was usually the primary weapon since it had a longer reach than the sword. Other staff weapons were also carried. The halberd consisted of a large blade backed by a hook and topped by a spike. Many lesser soldiers were armed with the bill. This was derived from the agricultural implement, but had the addition of a side hook and top spike. The so-called 'brown bill' was a peculiarly English weapon. Other weapons might also have been seen, but were probably more rare. The glaive was essentially a long convex blade mounted on a haft; the Welsh hook was rather like a scythe with side projections.

Large numbers of archers were present on the battlefield. The English longbow had by this time earned a reputation for itself. Carried in the hands of men trained from boyhood, it was a lethal weapon and had spelled ruin for a number of French armies who tried to advance against it. Now against other English armies also equipped with bowmen, the archers often tended to cancel each other out. Neither side wanted to stand and endure the deadly showers of arrows for long, and preferred to close for hand-to-hand combat. The bow itself was as tall as a man, and usually made from imported Spanish or Italian yew, tipped with nocks of horn for the hempen string. The draw weight is estimated to have been well over 80lbs, and many would have been about 120lbs. The arrows might be of ash or sometimes poplar, usually fletched with goose

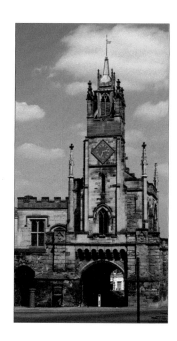

The 15th-century East Gate of Warwick with St Peter's Chapel on top. When Edward arrived in the town on his march from Yorkshire he at last openly proclaimed himself king. He then rode out with Richard to greet Clarence before heading south for London on about 3 April.

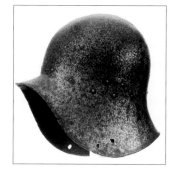

A *sallet* or perhaps kettle hat, made in the second half of the 15th century perhaps in Milan. It was probably made for export to west Europe. (By courtesy of the Trustees of the Armouries, IV.4)

feathers. Arrowheads came in several forms. Large broad heads, some with long swallow-tailed barbs, were essentially for hunting, designed to stick in an animal and cut blood vessels with the long sharp edges, but they could equally be used to shoot horses. Being large and seldom wearing much armour other than a steel shaffron or cloth caparison, the arrows could easily shear through flesh and bring an animal down. The fact that horses made easy targets was one reason for the decline in cavalry and why they were seldom ridden head-on against archers. Bodkins were quadrangular in section and narrow, probably designed to punch through mail rings. General-purpose heads were smaller and sometimes carried small barbs; some were reinforced with steel and seem to have been designed for punching through plate armour. Arrows were made in their thousands. Each archer carried a sheaf, usually 24 shafts, either tucked in his belt or in a cloth bag. Additional sheaves were carried by baggage wagons.

Firearms

Guns played a part at both Barnet and Tewkesbury. The handgun at this time consisted of a tube with a touch-hole at the breech. It was muzzle loading, and provided either with a wooden stock or else an iron rod. It was fired by touching a hot iron or piece of smouldering match cord to loose priming powder at the touch-hole, which in turn ignited the charge in the barrel. These guns fired small lead balls carried in a bag by the gunner. The *Great Chronicle of London* describes the foreign hand-gunners as sooty, presumably a description of their smoky clothes and faces grimy from the smoke and flash of the priming powder.

Artillery pieces featured in both armies at both battles. These were presumably the light field pieces borne on wheeled carriages, rather than the heavy siege ordnance that crawled along behind a team of straining oxen or horses, and which would have been far too slow for Edward's purposes. Field guns were often breech-loaders, utilising a chamber filled with gunpowder that could be secured in place by hammering a wedge behind it, though the fit allowed gases to escape. However, it meant that several chambers could be kept at hand for relatively quick reloading. Metal bands might secure the barrel to a split trail, the top half pivoting to elevate or depress the muzzle. The guns fired solid cut stone balls, but it is known that a type of canister shot was in use at this time, as well as star shells. There is no evidence for either at Barnet or Tewkesbury. Star shells would have exposed the actual position of the Yorkists at Barnet, which was not discovered. Had one side possessed quantities of canister it might have won them the battle.

Size of the armies

As to the size of the armies, on commenting on how God favoured Edward's forces at Barnet the *Arrivall* states:

> And it is to wit, that it could not be judged, that the King's host 'passed in number nine thousand men; but such a Great and Gracious Lord, is Almighty God, that it pleaseth him [to] give the victory, as well to [the] *few, as to* [the] *many.*

This is a reasonable size given the tendency to exaggeration common among medieval chroniclers. However, it also says there were 30,000 Lancastrians, which seems unlikely. Warworth mentions 7,000 with Edward on Good Friday. Von Wesel, who witnessed the Yorkist muster, gives a figure of 15,000, and Waurin 20,000. Thus a total of perhaps 12,000–15,000 men for Edward and a slightly larger number for Warwick may be correct. Von Wesel estimated the Lancastrians had some 3,000 more men than the Yorkists.

At Tewkesbury Edward fielded a much smaller army. Payments for 3,436 archers after the battle, given that armies often comprised a majority of archers, suggests perhaps only 5,000–6,000 men. The *Arrivall* says Edward had 3,000 footmen, but many, including a number of archers, rode to battle, even if they then dismounted. The Lancastrian force at Tewkesbury was perhaps larger than the Yorkist by a few hundred men.

THE MARCH TO BARNET

Having left Flushing, Edward's invasion fleet headed for Norfolk. Towards the evening of Tuesday, 12 March, they arrived off Cromer, and Sir Robert Chamberlain and Sir Gilbert Debenham were sent ashore with a number of others to assess the possibilities of a landing. They discovered from allies, however, that Richard of Warwick, and the Earl of Oxford in particular, controlled the interior and it was not reckoned safe to make landfall. Warwick had sent letters of privy seal to all gentlemen whom he suspected, 'and put in ward about London or else found surety'. The Duke of Norfolk was out of the area. Edward decided to head north. On the night of 13 March and into the following morning of the 14th, storms arose to hamper the fleet's progress. During the day it arrived off the Humber estuary, but the ships were forced apart by the strong winds and heavy seas. Edward's ship, in which, says the *Arrivall*, were also Lord Hastings, his chamberlain, and 500 chosen troops, came to Ravenspur at the mouth of the River Humber, the same place at which Henry Bolingbroke had set foot on his way to becoming Henry IV in 1399. Richard of Gloucester with a company of 300 men landed some four miles away, while Earl Rivers with 200 men landed 14 miles away at Powle. Other ships were also dispersed. Edward spent the night in an unimpressive village with his company, while during the hours of darkness and the next morning, as the winds abated, his scattered forces gradually came together.

Though at a reasonably safe distance from any immediate threat, the area chosen for the landing also meant that Edward had a long march to reach the more pro-Yorkist south of England. Certainly few from the vicinity showed much enthusiasm to give their support. Stowe says a priest named Westerdale actually opposed the king. Edward discussed what they should do next. The direct route against his enemies lay towards London and the south, but this would mean crossing the Humber, something the *Arrivall* says was abhorrent to Edward's followers, as well as making it appear that Edward was withdrawing through fear, 'which note of slander they were right loath to suffer'. In order to put his mark on the area, therefore, Edward then set off, not south, but northwest towards the unpredictable city of York. The county itself was full of

The garter stall plate of William, Lord Hastings. (Reproduced by permission of the Dean and Canons of Windsor)

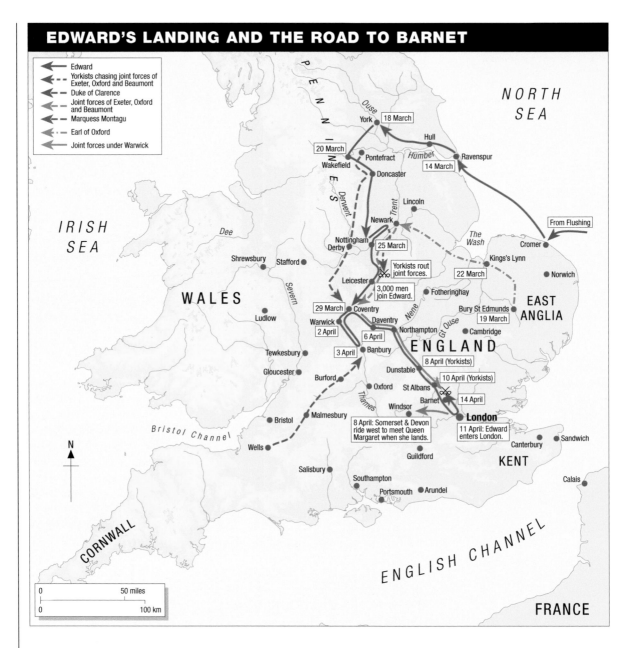

Lancastrians, many armed bands, especially a dangerous group under Martin de la See from Barmston in Holderness. The first town Edward reached was Kingston upon Hull, which snubbed him. He moved on towards York, where he arrived on 18 March. Though he did not encounter overt hostility, Edward was only allowed to enter with a handful of men. He left the city on 20 March and headed for Sandal Castle to the south of Wakefield, scene of his father's disastrous defeat and death almost 11 years earlier. The first real threat lay ahead. A few miles from Sandal stood the powerful Pontefract Castle, and there was a real danger that from here Montagu might launch an attack on Edward's little band. However, nothing happened. Even the author of the *Arrivall* admits that he did not know why Montagu remained aloof, commenting that he liked to think it was from goodwill. He also points out, however, that Montagu was

The moat enclosing the site of Old Fold Manor to the west of the St Albans road. Once a medieval manor house that witnessed the Battle of Barnet, it is now occupied by a golf course.

also probably following the will of his powerful neighbour, the Earl of Northumberland. Percy was not antagonistic towards Edward – he had after all done well from him, being restored to his earldom the previous year – yet nor could he actively do much to assist him in an area where too many Lancastrian sympathisers remembered Edward's bloody victory at Towton only ten years before. However, by allowing Edward to march away unhindered, the *Arrivall* notes, Percy did him 'right good and notable service'. Perhaps surprisingly, the *Arrivall* comments that, on Edward's arrival at Sandal Castle, fewer people than might be supposed bothered to come in to him, and he must have been a disappointed man to encounter such indifference. However, as Edward marched south, things began to change. William Dudley came in with some men at Doncaster, while Sir William Parr and Sir James Harrington brought 600 men from Lancashire

A probably medieval hedge running towards the St Albans road, perhaps one that Lancastrian troops sheltered behind the night before the Battle of Barnet.

31

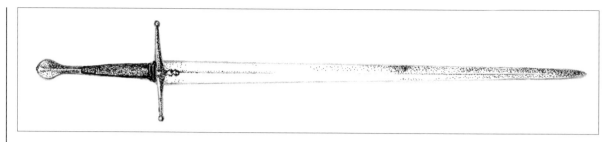

and the surrounding areas when Edward arrived at Nottingham. At Leicester a sizeable contingent of 3,000 troops from Lord Hastings joined, under command of Sir William Stanley and Sir William Norris. The increasing size of the Yorkist forces was apposite, for Edward now learned that Newark was occupied by sizeable Lancastrian forces (the *Arrivall* says 4,000) under the Duke of Exeter, the Earl of Oxford, and William, formerly Viscount Beaumont. However, notwithstanding, Edward took the initiative and marched his men from Nottingham towards the enemy forces. However, there was to be no confrontation; the Lancastrians, unwilling to face him, had left Newark at about two o'clock in the morning and were heading south to join the Earl of Warwick. The latter was meanwhile moving through his county trying to recruit troops. Edward was still threatened, for Montagu had now stirred into action and was marching south towards him. Edward, who had returned to Nottingham, resolved to keep ahead of Montagu and left Nottingham, heading now for Coventry via Leicester. Whilst at Leicester some 3,000 men, well armed, arrived in response to messages sent by Lord Hastings. Warwick, on learning of the enemy advance, retired into Coventry and closed the gates, so that when the Yorkists arrived Edward faced a siege. He tried to mediate, offering Warwick a free pardon for himself and his followers, which was refused. According to the French version of the *Arrivall*, Exeter and Oxford now launched an attack but it was successfully beaten off. It was this uncoordinated strike, and the reluctance of Warwick to fight, that saved Edward from what could have been a very tight situation. Had Montagu liaised with Warwick and with Exeter's followers while the Yorkists lay in Nottingham, Edward might well have found himself facing assault from three directions at once. It never happened, and now the weakness of Warwick resulted in another gain for the Yorkists; Edward's brother, the Duke of Clarence, deserted Warwick's cause. Edward moved to Warwick, and on 2 April learned that his brother was approaching from Burford. Together with Richard of Gloucester, he rode out next day and the three brothers met on the Banbury road. Now bolstered by the addition of Clarence's troops, Edward again challenged Richard of Warwick to come out of Coventry, but to no avail. Clarence was sent to mediate and hammer out honourable terms of surrender, but got nowhere. Faced with an obdurate enemy whom he was incapable of besieging, Edward withdrew on 5 April and turned south. Now he headed for London, hoping to win over more men to his standards, at the same time confronting King Henry and frightening Lancastrian adherents who blocked aid.

It was a gamble, for Warwick was still at large behind him, but Edward pressed on. The Duke of Somerset, Marquis of Dorset and Earl of Devon had moved up to London but in April turned south and reached the coast in hope of a rendezvous with Queen Margaret and

A two-hand sword, possibly English, about 1450.

A pollaxe of about 1430, perhaps of German manufacture, with axe blade, hammer and spike. The cheeks extending down the haft protect it from being cut through by an opponents weapon.

Prince Edward. The latter, together with the Countess of Warwick and others, had boarded their ships on 24 March in the hope of striking at the south-west coast of Britain. They stayed in the ships until 13 April, foiled by strong winds and high seas.

Marching via Daventry, Edward reached Northampton. As he marched on, he was careful, notes the *Arrivall*, always to leave behind him:

> *a good band of spears and archers* [for] *his behind-riders to 'counter, if it needed, such of the Earl's party, as, peradventure, he should have sent to have troubled him on the backhalfe, if he so had done.*

Edward moved down Watling Street through Dunstable, reaching St Albans on 10 April. At his approach London was in turmoil. Messages from Edward were echoed by messages from Warwick. Powerful Yorkists such as the Earl of Essex stirred up sympathisers, while the confounded mayor took refuge in his bed. Archbishop Neville and Lord Sudeley were the only men of note to support Henry in the City, and on 9 April they decided to parade the wretched king to drum up support, Neville holding his hand and Henry dressed in a long blue velvet gown, 'as though he had no more to change with', says the *Great Chronicle*. This sorry sight had almost the reverse effect, and there was little evidence of resistance. Apart from the threat of damage to the City, which would affect mercantile profits, some richer Londoners wanted to recoup loans made to Edward, while Commines tells us that a number of ladies, remembering relationships with the young king, also influenced decisions. The Tower of London was taken for the king, and it was decided to let Edward enter unmolested.

Edward IV leading his army, with a pile of corpses in evidence. The two armoured figures to his left carry pollaxes, and most wear *sallets*. Edward's standard of the Black Bull of Clarence, perhaps in simplified form, can be seen above his head slightly to right of centre. (By permission of the British Library, Ms Harley 7353)

Edward entered London on 11 April. The *Great Chronicle* remarked on 500 'black and smoky sort of Flemish gunners', handgunners who marched at the head of the Yorkist army. Edward paused at St Paul's to make offering, then made for the bishop's palace and the person of King Henry. They shook hands, then Henry, together with the Archbishop of York and several bishops, was led to the Tower. Edward went to Westminster for a crown-wearing ceremony and at last greeted his wife in the sanctuary, together with Edward, the five-month-old son he had never seen, the future boy-king Edward V. The following day, Good Friday, men began to arrive in London to join Edward's cause. Even as numbers swelled his ranks, Edward learned that Warwick was marching against him and had reached St Albans. The *Arrivall* says that the Earl hoped that Edward had been blocked by the Londoners and refused entry, but if not, then the Earl intended to surprise his enemies in London during the Easter festivities. This may be true, but Edward did not wait to find out.

Taking Henry VI with him, Edward marched out of London the following day, Saturday 13 April. As well as Gloucester and Clarence, he was backed by several powerful nobles, including Hastings and his brother, Sir Ralph Hastings, John, Lord Howard, and Humphrey Bourchier, Lord Cromwell. By evening his journey up the

Monken Hadley church, looking north, on the east side of the battlefield at Barnet. The church does not appear to have been built until after the battle, but a hermitage seems to have stood in the vicinity.

Great North Road had brought him near the market town of Barnet, which lay along the route. Warwick had moved down from St Albans and, marching via South Mimms and Kitts End, had approached Barnet from the north. The Yorkist 'aforeriders' came into the streets and clashed sharply with their Lancastrian counterparts. After a short struggle the Lancastrians were chased out of Barnet, galloping northwards, hotly pursued by the Yorkists. Riding up the road, the latter suddenly came upon a dark monster stretched endlessly across the road in the gathering gloom. It was the main Lancastrian army ordering its ranks and partly concealed by hedges, on a ridge that straddled the road about half a mile beyond the town. The Yorkists turned their mounts and rode back to warn Edward. On learning of the enemy position from his scourers, Edward decided to carry on through the town and out into the open fields to the north, refusing to let any man loiter in Barnet itself. By now darkness was falling but, undaunted, the Yorkist forces marched through the streets and out towards the enemy lines. As they closed to within gunshot, Edward decided, unusually, to form their order of battle ready for the following morning, presumably to launch an early attack. It was an interesting plan. He had reckoned without the darkness and the weather, however.

THE BATTLE OF BARNET

The location that was to become the battlefield of Barnet formed the highest ground between London and York. The Great North Road ran down from the north along a strip of open ridge some 200 yards wide, but not wide enough for a substantial force of men to form up easily. It was joined from the west by the road running south past Kitts End from St Albans. A little further south at Hadley, about half a mile north of the town of Barnet itself, the road crossed a ridge that extends both left and right of the highway, this being an ideal area for deploying troops in line. Near the road on its west side just north of this ridge was a moated residence known as Old Fold Manor. The *Arrivall* mentions a hedge under which the Lancastrians settled the night before battle; one possible candidate now runs east–west from the road. These hedges were probably quite thick and substantial, perhaps with accompanying drainage ditches, and studded with trees. Much of the rest of the ground was open heath land, then called Gladsmuir Heath but now known as Hadley Common. It is possible that some of the hedges survive, for a number can be seen on the western part of the field, now part of a golf club. At least one hedge is certainly older than the battle itself, but the hedge likely to be the one behind which the Lancastrians sheltered is difficult to date as it is not as well preserved and not enough plant species have survived to make accurate dating possible. The ditches running parallel either side of the hedge have not yielded any medieval material either. To the east of the road a track led from the Great North Road towards Enfield. Today it passes Monken Hadley Church, but in 1471 the church as it stands did not exist. However, it appears that there was some

A view south looking up towards the left rear of the Lancastrian position on the tree-lined ridge at Barnet.

sort of hermitage on the site, part of the endowment of the Benedictine monastery at Walden in Essex. The hermitage was set in a park – Enfield Chase – though not a park in the modern sense.

In the darkness Edward's men were marshalled quietly, forming up to oppose the enemy line. Part of the Lancastrian army over on the western side was positioned behind one of the hedges. In the darkness Edward failed to position his line properly with the result that his right flank over-lapped the enemy left, and vice versa. Not only this, he had deployed his men closer to the enemy than he probably intended, but in the darkness this went unnoticed. As it turned out, the close proximity of the armies worked to the Yorkists' advantage. Warwick trained his artillery pieces and opened fire, but in the darkness the balls howled over the army to fall harmlessly in rear, where the Earl expected his enemy to be lying. Edward wisely issued orders that no guns, or very few, were to fire back at the Lancastrians, and instructed his troops to remain quiet, so that Warwick would not realise his mistake and order his gunners to depress their muzzles. Indeed, the guns fired through the night, the gunners blissfully ignorant of the lack of damage they were inflicting, though it must have made sleep difficult for either army. In any case the *Arrivall* informs us that Edward had his whole force up and ready for action at sometime between four and five o'clock in the morning, before it was properly light (Von Wesel and *Warkworth's Chronicle* say the battle started at 4.00am). Edward now faced another problem, however. Though sunrise on that Easter Sunday, 14 April, was at about 5.00am, a thick mist had descended, soaking the soldiers and reducing the visibility. A story later arose that it had been produced by the incantations of a Friar Bungay!

The *Arrivall* only mentions the King's battle and the Earl's battle, and does not distinguish the divisions of any other commander. If the author was indeed a priest at the rear with the baggage, it suggests either that he did not bother to note how the divisions were set out, or that from where he was placed he could not see them properly in the dark and then the fog. The Yorkist line appears to have been formed across the road in the traditional three battles, a total of some 12,000–15,000 men. Edward himself commanded the central division. To the east stood the division under Richard of Gloucester, overlapping the enemy flank, while Lord Hastings commanded the left, itself overlapped by the division opposed to it. Holinshed also mentions that:

> *beside these three battles, he kept a company of fresh men in store, which did him great pleasure before the end of the battle.*

The Lancastrians were also marshalled into three battles of perhaps 15,000–20,000 men. In the centre stood Richard, Earl of Warwick, with Montagu. To his left was the division of the Duke of Exeter, though Holinshed places Warwick with him, giving the centre mistakenly to the Duke of Somerset (who was at that time marching to join Margaret in the west country) and who according to Holinshed commanded archers set between the other divisions. To the west was the third Lancastrian division under the Earl of Oxford ('with certain horsemen', says Holinshed, who also mentions Montagu in this division). It partly overlapped that of Hastings and was protected to some degree by the thick hedge. Monken Hadley church marks roughly where the eastern end of the Lancastrian

The hilt of a 15th-century thrusting sword. Note the pronounced medial rib that stiffens the pointed blade for a thrust. (By courtesy of the Trustees of the Armouries, IX.)

line stood, then running west along the ridge across the road and passing to the south of Old Fold Manor. Both armies had formed up largely on foot, the warhorses of many men-at-arms probably tethered in rear at a convenient distance should they be required swiftly for pursuit or flight.

Before battle commenced Edward had given the command for 'No quarter', now ignoring his previous comments at Towton that his policy was to kill the lords and spare the common soldiers. The mist concealed much of the scene from the soldiery, many of whom had no idea what their comrades several yards away were doing, and most being unaware of the potentially lethal overlap at each end of the line.

The attack began very early in the morning, perhaps at seven o'clock, the mist at this hour giving no hint of lifting. Cannon on both sides opened fire with stone shot, while handgunners, particularly in Edward's army, added to the cacophony of noise, and the more silent archers did their deadly work. Casualties were inflicted, but as archers and gunners were busy on both sides, the results do not seem to have given either army an advantage. Eager to close and get away from the missiles, to which they had no reply, the men-at-arms were no doubt relieved when Edward gave the order for a general advance along the whole line. The limited visibility must have hampered a concerted attack and the two sides may have come together in rather piecemeal fashion. On the western side, the hedges particularly hampered the Yorkists, who, says the *Arrivall*, had to cut their way through to get to grips with their opponents. Here, however, the fact that Oxford's division extended well beyond the Yorkist line proved decisive. As his troops swung in on the flanks as well as the front of Hastings' division, the Yorkists eventually decided they were getting into a dangerously compacted situation, one from which it would soon become impossible to extricate themselves. A few men broke away and fled into the mist southwards away from the fighting. Then large parts of the division began to crumble. Soon hundreds of men were running back towards Barnet town. Whether ordered to or not, Oxford's men gave chase, cutting down any stragglers. The fugitives, meanwhile, were flooding into the town, running through the high street and out the other end and on down the road. Some did not stop until they reached London, where they cried it abroad that the battle was lost; this news then reached the Continent before it could be corrected. Other fugitives veered off to seek safety in the more wooded ground, greatly assisted by the dense mist. Oxford's men now streamed into Barnet as they raged through the town hunting out enemy soldiers. Once this was complete, many of them fell to looting the place. Others passed through the town, moving south over a stone causeway a mile further on. De Vere and his captains came up and tried with difficulty to marshal their troops, knowing that the battle was far from over. Men were fired up by blood lust and many were keen to steal from the houses to augment their wages. By a great effort de Vere managed to rally together some 800 of them (according to Warworth's comment on his later flight), and now cajoled and willed them back up the road towards the fighting, somewhere ahead of them through the murk.

The Battle of Barnet, as portrayed in the late 15th-century Ghent version of *The Arrivall of Edward IV*. The building on the promontory is probably meant to represent Old Fold Manor. (Universiteit Bibliotheek, Ghent, Ms 264)

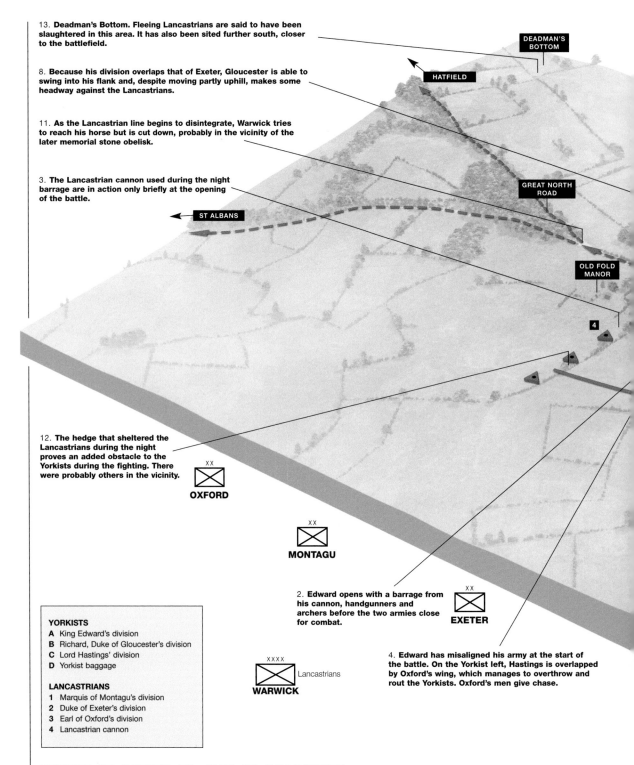

13. Deadman's Bottom. Fleeing Lancastrians are said to have been slaughtered in this area. It has also been sited further south, closer to the battlefield.

8. Because his division overlaps that of Exeter, Gloucester is able to swing into his flank and, despite moving partly uphill, makes some headway against the Lancastrians.

11. As the Lancastrian line begins to disintegrate, Warwick tries to reach his horse but is cut down, probably in the vicinity of the later memorial stone obelisk.

3. The Lancastrian cannon used during the night barrage are in action only briefly at the opening of the battle.

DEADMAN'S BOTTOM

HATFIELD

GREAT NORTH ROAD

ST ALBANS

OLD FOLD MANOR

4

12. The hedge that sheltered the Lancastrians during the night proves an added obstacle to the Yorkists during the fighting. There were probably others in the vicinity.

X X
OXFORD

X X
MONTAGU

2. Edward opens with a barrage from his cannon, handgunners and archers before the two armies close for combat.

X X
EXETER

X X X X Lancastrians
WARWICK

4. Edward has misaligned his army at the start of the battle. On the Yorkist left, Hastings is overlapped by Oxford's wing, which manages to overthrow and rout the Yorkists. Oxford's men give chase.

YORKISTS
A King Edward's division
B Richard, Duke of Gloucester's division
C Lord Hastings' division
D Yorkist baggage

LANCASTRIANS
1 Marquis of Montagu's division
2 Duke of Exeter's division
3 Earl of Oxford's division
4 Lancastrian cannon

THE BATTLE OF BARNET

14 April 1471, 6.00–7.00am, viewed from the south-west showing how the misaligned deployments of the previous night lead to the rout of the Yorkist left and the pivoting of the battle lines anti-clockwise. As Oxford returns to the battle he is fired on by his own side in a case of mistaken identity and the Lancastrian line begins to disintegrate. The Earl of Warwick is killed as he flees the field.

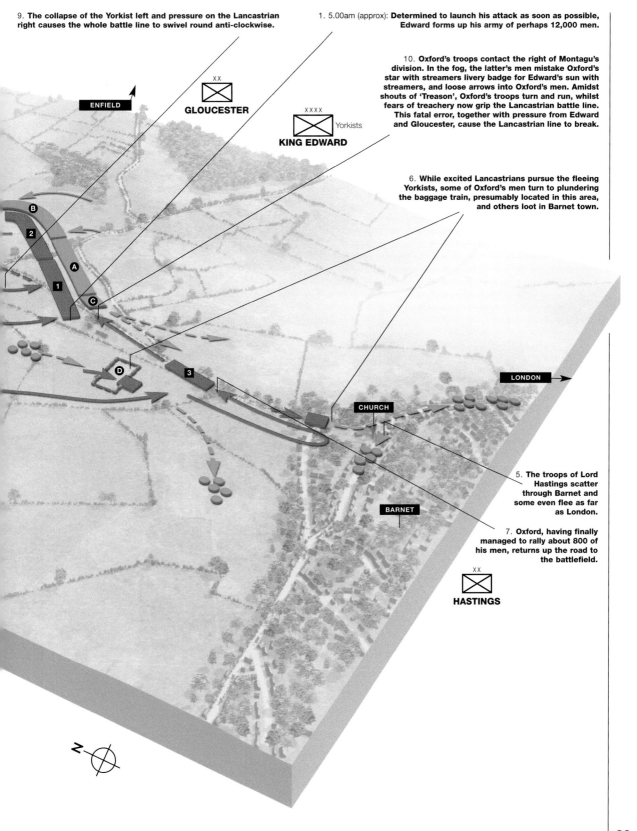

9. The collapse of the Yorkist left and pressure on the Lancastrian right causes the whole battle line to swivel round anti-clockwise.

1. 5.00am (approx): Determined to launch his attack as soon as possible, Edward forms up his army of perhaps 12,000 men.

10. Oxford's troops contact the right of Montagu's division. In the fog, the latter's men mistake Oxford's star with streamers livery badge for Edward's sun with streamers, and loose arrows into Oxford's men. Amidst shouts of 'Treason', Oxford's troops turn and run, whilst fears of treachery now grip the Lancastrian battle line. This fatal error, together with pressure from Edward and Gloucester, cause the Lancastrian line to break.

6. While excited Lancastrians pursue the fleeing Yorkists, some of Oxford's men turn to plundering the baggage train, presumably located in this area, and others loot in Barnet town.

5. The troops of Lord Hastings scatter through Barnet and some even flee as far as London.

7. Oxford, having finally managed to rally about 800 of his men, returns up the road to the battlefield.

ENFIELD

GLOUCESTER

KING EDWARD

Yorkists

LONDON

CHURCH

BARNET

HASTINGS

N

39

Aerial view of Barnet battlefield. The town of Barnet is just visible at the top of the picture, with the A1000 running down from the town and the modern A1081 feeding in from the middle right edge of the picture. In the centre of the picture the Great North Road forks to the left, Kitt's End Road to the right. The memorial stone sits just below this junction. Above, the narrow triangle of roads marks the position of Gladmore Heath, now Hadley Common. The road running slightly up from the left of the triangle is Drury Road and leads past Monken Hadley church and marks the rough position of the Lancastrian left wing, while just below the junction on the other side of the A1000 is the golf course, with Old Fold Manor and possible early hedge line above.

In his interpretation, Sir James Ramsey made the mistake of placing the hedge alongside the main road to Hatfield. This then caused him to place Warwick's army along it facing east. This could be explained by the confusion when Oxford returned and fell on the Lancastrian flank. It was also widely suggested by early 20th-century historians that, on his return, Oxford became lost in the fog and simply veered too far west before turning in on the flank of the Lancastrian division. Burne had already discounted this theory in 1950. It does seem rather improbable that, having charged down the road into Barnet and out across the causeway, de Vere was incapable of finding his way back up the same road, across which two large armies were ranged. Even if his main force had swung wide of the road itself during their attack, his men could not fail to find it as it left the town. What is far more likely to have happened is that, as a result of the overlapping effect at both ends and the obvious advantage this gave to the division that could then swing in on the enemy flank, the battle lines had pivoted counter-clockwise as both the Yorkist left and Lancastrian right gave ground under the pressure. On the eastern side, Gloucester would have probably found himself initially marching downhill and then up towards Exeter's division. The ground may have been soft and muddy, perhaps marshy. His troops may possibly have had to negotiate the walls of the hermitage on the site of Monken Hadley church, swirling around them to regroup beyond as they made for their enemies. Richard would have discovered that part of the

Hadley Common, looking north. Once called Gladmore Heath, this was open scrubland at the time of the battle and probably formed the centre of the lines that fanned out either side. The St Albans road runs north on the left.

Lancastrian division was not in front of him as expected, and his men would then have to swing slowly left until they appeared out of the fog. In the confusion the Yorkists probably did not have much chance to press home a violent flank attack before Exeter's men realised where their opponents were and did their best to swing themselves about to try to meet the onslaught head on. Once they made contact, Richard does not seem to have been able to make as much headway as Oxford on the other flank, but the two armies most probably now lined up on a more north-east to south-west axis.

As Oxford came up the road, he began to make out figures in the mist. At the same time men in the Lancastrian centre spotted troops looming out of the murk. Probably largely unaware of the debacle on the Yorkist left wing, the men of Warwick's division looked for some sign of recognition. Then it was noticed that men wore emblems that looked like the sunburst badge of King Edward and, assuming that these were Yorkist reinforcements, the archers in Warwick's division nocked their arrows and sent some well-aimed volleys into them. As *Warkworth's Chronicle* explains:

> But it happened so, that the Earl of Oxford's men had upon them their lord's livery, both before and behind, which was a star with streams, which [was] much like King Edward's livery, the sun with streams.

Amidst howls of pain and rage, the troops that Oxford had rallied shouted 'Treason', believing that Warwick's men had changed sides as had happened with other lords in the climate of the times. Some no doubt shot arrows back, others decided the day must be lost if many of their own side had gone over to the enemy, and fled the field, according to *Warkworth's Chronicle* taking some 800 men from the battle. As shouts of betrayal ran through the Lancastrian ranks, unease spread. In the thick mist the soldiers could not see what was happening further down the lines; in such conditions any cry of treason must have been deeply unsettling, especially as former enemies now fought on the same side. At about the same time Gloucester pressed hard on Exeter's division in

BARNET – A CASE OF MISTAKEN IDENTITY (pages 42-43)
After the rout of the Yorkist left, the Earl of Oxford managed to round up perhaps 800 of his pursuing troops and lead them back up towards the battlefield. Meanwhile it seems likely that the fighting lines had swung counter-clockwise. Here men in the central division under the Marquis of Montagu, now lacking Oxford's division on their right, spot troops looming out of the mist. The central figure is Montagu, wearing a tabard bearing his family arms, whose complexity bears out the intermarriage of powerful families (1). He differenced his paternal Neville saltire with a label compony; the quartered fusils (tall diamonds) and green displayed eagles are for Montagu and Monthermer respectively. On the centre of these arms he has placed an inescutcheon bearing the arms of his wife, Isobel Inglethorp. He is further marked out by the banner borne aloft behind him. Though much of his armour is concealed, he wears a west European harness with a tall, visored sallet with a decorative finial on top. His chin and throat are protected by a pivoting bevor, the latter strapped round his neck at the rear. He lifts a pollaxe, an axe blade backed by a hammer and topped with a quadrilateral spike. The long steel langets help protect the haft from being cut, while the rondel or disk help prevent a weapon sliding down on to his hand. The man to the right of Montagu, probably one of his knightly

retainers, wears similar amour but the bevor has no pivoting upper part (2). The bolt securing the reinforcing plate to each shoulder defence can be seen. The overlapping steel scales that guard the fingers are also visible. To the left of Montagu a retainer wears a collection of pieces perhaps acquired by various means (3). His basic protection is a sleeved 'jack', consisting of numerous layers of linen all stitched in squares to keep it in place. In this case the sleeves are reinforced by the addition of pieces of chain stitched down the arms, and he has also acquired couters to guard his elbows. More importantly, a breastplate gives solid protection to his chest; it is buckled to a backplate behind. The plackart over his stomach doubles protection in an area where wounds usually proved fatal due to material in the digestive tract poisoning the system. He wears a less enclosing style of sallet, secured by a chinstrap. Behind, an archer points at the oncoming troops. He carries his arrows tucked into his belt (4). He and the soldier at far right (5) are each well protected by a front-fastening brigandine. The rivet heads hold numerous small plates behind a canvas jacket, though this is covered by richer cloth to make it more attractive; both have open sallets. The banners in the distance are those of the Earl of Oxford but, due to the fog, the stars will be misinterpreted as the suns in splendour of Yorkist Edward, with fatal consequences (6). (Graham Turner)

44

A cannonball, one of several found on Hadley Green. Unfortunately they all appear to be of 19th-century date, when an army display was held on the common.

front and flank, slowly pushing them back. In the centre Edward, who may have got an idea of the disarray in the enemy ranks, pressed the attack despite the damage to his left wing. To make matters worse for the Lancastrians, Montagu had been killed. The *Arrivall* says he was slain 'in plain battle'. *Warkworth's Chronicle* describes him wearing King Edward's livery and being slain by one of Warwick's men, but there is no other evidence he had changed sides. On the contrary, Sir John Paston makes mention of his conduct at Barnet, as does the Continuator of Hardyng's Chronicle, who had accused him of treachery before the battle. Perhaps the panic caused by the confusion and shouts of treason may have been his undoing. The enemy wavered and then broke. Some ran up the St Albans road towards Kitts End, or along the Great North Road; others fled down the rear slopes of the ridge and out over the rough heath land, probably seeking woody country which might give them safety from pursuing horsemen.

Warwick must have realised that all was lost; his brother was dead (*Warkworth's Chronicle* says it was his death that prompted Warwick to flee; Holinshed says Warwick died while Montagu was trying to help him) and de Vere had fled. Warwick is said to have mounted his horse and ridden off northwards towards Barnet wood, 'somewhat flying' as the *Arrivall* has it. *Warkworth's Chronicle* tells how he discovered that there was no obvious way through the wood, and while thus delayed he was set upon by Yorkist soldiers, dragged to the ground and killed. By the time Edward hurried to the scene he was too late to intervene and save him, Warwick's body had been stripped of its armour and lay naked on the grass. The stone memorial set up to commemorate the battle in 1740 was supposed to mark the approximate place of his death. He may alternatively have been caught in the vicinity of Wrotham Park. Holinshed makes the interesting comment that Warwick's usual battle practice was to ride from place to place encouraging his men, but at Barnet the fighting was so fierce that Montagu advised him to dismount and actually fight. He additionally asserts that some said Edward also was constrained that day to fight in his own person, which sounds more like a dig at a Yorkist. Having then noted Warwick as dying in the press, he remarks that some said he had been caught as he fled. Victorian writers were sometimes loath to believe that the Kingmaker was not 'the bravest man of a brave age', and attack those contemporaries mentioned above as biased for daring to suggest otherwise. The author of the *Arrivall*, for example, is damned as 'evidently not a fighting man', though what that has to do with spotting whether or not someone is running away is questionable. Some Victorians believed the Earl rushed to check the panic as the Lancastrian right broke up and Edward stormed in at the centre, the earl falling covered with wounds. In the best Hollywood tradition one story has him confronted by Richard of Gloucester, the man whom he nurtured as a boy. The Earl, mindful of his promise to the dying Duke of York, spares his arm and a few minutes later is slain by Richard, while Montagu rushes up and also perishes.

The battle had probably lasted about three hours – so says the *Arrivall*, though *Warkworth's Chronicle* says it ended at 10.00am after saying it began at 4.00am – and had been a hard-fought killing-match. Despite his victory Edward's army had taken some notable casualties. Lord Say and Lord Cromwell were both dead, as was Sir Humphrey Bourchier and Sir William Blount, heir to Lord Mountjoy. Apart from Warwick and

Standards of Edward IV. The top flag has white rose *en soleil* plus several smaller ones. The bottom flag bears a golden lion, with six red roses on blue and six white roses on red. he seems to have used this standard after his marriage to the Lancastrian Elizabeth Woodville. (College of Arms, Ms I.2, p.17)

Montagu the Lancastrians had not lost any nobles of rank, though Exeter was badly wounded and lay out on the battlefield, despoiled, naked and left for dead. *Warkworth's Chronicle* says he lay there from seven in the morning until four in the afternoon, until somebody realised he was alive. He was taken to a house that Leland notes was called Rutheland, by a man of his own following, where a leech attended his wounds and he was afterwards taken into sanctuary at Westminster. He subsequently spent four years as a prisoner in the Tower. Sir William Tyrell and Sir Lewis Johns were killed, says Sir John Paston, 'And divers other Esquires of our country, Godmarston and Booth'.

The Earl of Oxford and his two brothers, and also Viscount Beaumont, made good their escape from the field and headed north, finally managing to reach Scotland. Sir John Paston and his brother, also John, had fought in Oxford's division, since the major landholder where

The church of St Mary the Virgin, Barnet, on the north side of the junction of the High Street with Wood Street. Yorkist refugees and Oxford's men must have swept past here during the rout of Hastings' division.

The area immediately north-west of Monken Hadley, where fleeing Lancastrians would have passed. It is one of the sites located as Deadman's Bottom.

The rolling country north of Monken Hadley, seen from the Great North Road, is another area identified as Deadman's Bottom.

they lived in Norfolk, the Yorkist Duke himself, had besieged their castle at Caister. In a letter home to his mother from London on the following Thursday, Sir John described how:

My brother John is alive and well, and in no danger of dying.
Nevertheless he is badly hurt by an arrow in his right arm below the
elbow, and I have sent a surgeon to him, who has dressed the wound;
and he tells me that he hopes he will be healed within a very short time.

This may have been a case of friendly fire. By 30 April John, now much better, wrote complaining of the cost of his treatment – £5 in a fortnight – and that he was penniless. He signed himself 'John of Geldeston' (his birthplace) and wrote no address on the outside, since he had not yet been pardoned.

Von Wesel gives the casualties in the battle as 1,500 'on both sides', suggesting he means 3,000 in all, a similar figure to that given by the

Great Chronicle. Commines also says 1,500 were killed on Edward's side. Stow (*Warkworth's Chronicle*) has 4,000 killed. Sir John Paston, who was present on Warwick's side, says: 'and other people of both parties to the number of more than a thousand'. Fabian's figure is 1,500, while Holinshed and Hall assert that 10,000 at least were slain on both sides.

Edward immediately returned to London. Henry VI was put back in the Tower, with a guard of what appears to be 36 men, on rota, later reduced to 22. He was provided with 'clothes, beds and other necessary items' as a record of payments notes. Edward took Warwick's banner, picked up after the battle, and striding into St Paul's, where the afternoon service was in progress, laid the banner on the high altar. Next day he had the bodies of Warwick and Montagu displayed naked on the pavement in St Paul's to make sure that everyone realised the pair were actually dead and did not believe 'fained seditious tales' that they were still alive. After three days (according to Fenn, *Warkworth's Chronicle* says 3 or 4) he had the corpses packed off to Bisham Abbey in Berkshire where they were interred in the family vault, rather than have them quartered and displayed on selected bridges or gates. Perhaps this was a final act of mercy for his one-time friend and tutor, though Grafton suggests the common people said that Edward was not so jocund for the death of Warwick but he was more sorrowful for that of Montagu, who had appeared to be his faithful friend. It was for Montagu's sake, according to this source, that the brothers were given decent burial.

A ring whose bezel bears a bear and ragged staff, said to have been found on the battlefield at Barnet. (City of Liverpool Museum)

THE MARCH TO TEWKESBURY

The same day that Edward triumphed at Barnet, Queen Margaret and her son, Prince Edward, landed at Weymouth with a small group of English and French fighting men. The following day, 15 April, she received news that Warwick had been killed at Barnet and his army scattered. At first she faltered. Was it really worth going on? Edward was not the man to allow her force to survive; if he could smash it, he would. Indeed it appeared a rather feeble army. As she dithered over whether to sail back to France, the Earl of Pembroke urged her to fight on, and agreed to raise an army in Wales. Others offered their support and promises of forces from Cheshire and Lancashire. The Queen decided to carry on.

Edward meanwhile had returned to London after refreshing his men. King Henry was placed back in the Tower. Two days after the battle, he learned that Margaret was back in England. On 19 April, Edward set up headquarters at Windsor as he waited for fresh troops to be collected there according to new summonses. Margaret moved from Weymouth and headed towards Exeter. She hoped to recruit sympathisers and to enlarge her forces by marching through Wales (hoping especially to liaise with Jasper Tudor, Earl of Pembroke, who had been sent a commission to raise troops) and northern England. As a diversion she sent patrols out towards Shaftesbury, thence to Salisbury, and from Wells via Bruton to Yeovil, to seek additional supporters and to create the illusion that she was actually heading for London.

Edward, having collected his army and ignoring the Lancastrian feints, had set out from Windsor and, marching through Abingdon, reached Cirencester by 30 April, by which date the Lancastrian army was at Bath. From Cirencester Edward could strike at Gloucester, which was 15 miles closer to him than it was to Margaret, and Gloucester was the nearest crossing place over the River Severn. However, Margaret now moved further from the city. On Wednesday, 1 May, she left Bath and turned west towards the port of Bristol, 12 miles distant. Edward thought this change of direction to be the result of his appearance, but it may well be that the Lancastrians hoped to find provisions and perhaps artillery pieces in Bristol. Their expectations were realised, and the Queen and her troops were received in friendship. However, she did not tarry in the city; Edward had wasted no time in marching a similar distance to Malmesbury the same day and Margaret knew she must cross the Severn as soon as possible. The direct route to Gloucester and the crossing point lay along the road across the plain, via Berkeley. However, this would soon be seen by Edward's scourers on the higher ground of the Cotswolds to the east. Edward would immediately move across and bar the way in the area around Berkeley, which lay five miles nearer to his army. A diversion must be arranged to fool the enemy into going the wrong way.

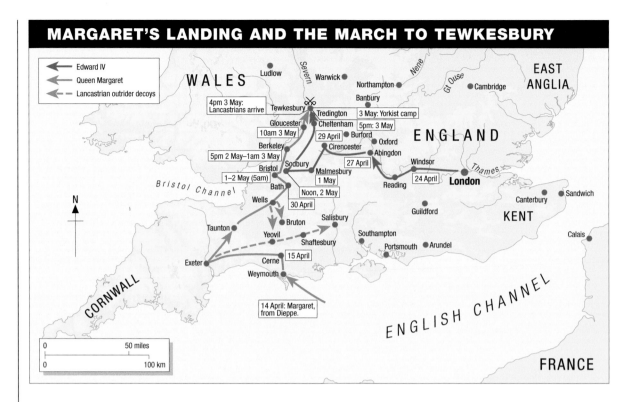

Early the following morning, 2 May, the Lancastrians marched towards Sodbury Hill, which lies on a southern spur of the Cotswolds midway between Malmesbury and Bristol.

Edward supposed that the enemy was about to make a stand in the area, and accordingly changed direction and made towards Sodbury. As the Yorkist scourers rode into the town on the lookout for bivouacs, they blundered into the Lancastrian out-riders. Some Yorkists were captured, others made off, no doubt recounting that the enemy was in possession of the town. Edward now fully expected a confrontation. He almost certainly slowed his march as he moved up towards Sodbury, awaiting news of the Lancastrian position. He reached Sodbury Hill about noon, only to find the place deserted. Margaret had completely outwitted him. By now the main Lancastrian force was moving towards Berkeley and passing west of Sodbury. Burne reconstructed this incident with the vanguard riding towards Sodbury as a feint, then pulling back latterly to protect the army's tail as a rearguard but the *Arrivall* makes no mention of such elaborations. The slight detour of perhaps three miles that this had cost Margaret was worth it; she had completely wrong-footed Edward, who had now marched well out of his way and lost the chance to cut her off. Now the Yorkists waited on Sodbury Hill, Edward no doubt fuming, while his scourers endeavoured to relocate the Lancastrians. He dare not make any rash moves in case the enemy was in the vicinity, and the *Arrivall* makes it plain that he thought it was. In fact it was now marching steadily on the 23 miles from Bristol to Berkeley, arriving in the latter village at about 6.00pm that evening. Edward, meanwhile, having decided the enemy had actually given him the slip, decided it was too late to do much about it, and made camp where he was on Sodbury Hill. Perhaps largely thanks to inadequate scouting, the Lancastrian army now had a 12-mile lead over the Yorkists.

The memorial stone, erected in 1740 at the fork of the St Albans road (which runs past to the left) and Great North Road. It may have been in this area that Warwick was caught and killed.

50

Pimlico House, set back on the west side of the St Albans Road, is said by tradition to stand on the site of the chapel erected to commemorate the dead.

The remains of the monastic range at Beaulieu Abbey, Hampshire. The Countess of Warwick took refuge at the abbey after the death of her husband at Barnet.

Anxious to keep the advantage thus gained, Margaret appears to have roused her troops very early the next morning – Burne suggested 1.00am. She well knew how quickly Edward could move when he wanted, and was probably edgy in case he now stole a march on her. Accordingly the Lancastrian army broke camp and set off on the last leg to Gloucester and the river crossing, some 14 miles distant. Two hours later a messenger came galloping up to Sodbury Hill and awakened Edward to tell him that the enemy was on the move from Berkeley and heading for Gloucester. The *Arrivall* says that Edward called a council of war, to discuss whether Margaret was making for Gloucester or Tewkesbury. Quite why he wasted time doing this is not obvious. The only course of action open to him was to follow the Lancastrians quickly, and the enemy's road was going to be the same whatever he decided to be their true course. His decision must be whether to drop down and chase the tail of the Lancastrians, or stay on the high ground and follow a roughly parallel course along the line of the Cotswolds. The council wisely decided on the latter course. It was more direct than taking the

time to move down on to the lower road, which was more wooded and almost certainly ploughed up somewhat by the passage of the enemy army. Burne noted Edward's indecision at this time; it is almost as if the detour the previous day had brought home to him that his judgement was not infallible, and his confidence had taken rather a hard knock. Nonetheless, it was decided to send messengers at top speed to warn the governor of Gloucester of Margaret's approach, and that Edward would soon be on hand to lend assistance. Once the army was ready, perhaps at 5.00am, it set out in battle order, with scourers riding ahead to probe for the enemy. So well did the Yorkist army move that the chronicle relates how the two armies were only five or six miles apart. This is a rather low figure considering the head start the Lancastrians had, and at best can surely only mean that the scouts and perhaps the first troops of the Yorkists were this distance from the rearmost soldiers of the Lancastrians.

Meanwhile the Yorkist gallopers had made good time and reached Gloucester ahead of the Lancastrian army. The town defences controlled the bridge over the River Severn. The governor, Sir Richard Beauchamp, received Edward's messengers and made sure the defences were manned and the gates closed. At perhaps 10.00am the Lancastrian army, weary from its 14-mile march, arrived before Gloucester only to find the city barred to them and the bridge with it. Angry and confused, the commanders threatened the town with an assault, but Sir Richard was not to be shifted. He well knew that the Lancastrians dare not delay for long, certainly not long enough to attack the city, for if they did so they would lay themselves wide open to a counterattack as soon as Edward appeared. After a pause while they considered their position, the Lancastrian army reluctantly moved off, now heading towards Tewkesbury. The next crossing place was one mile south of that town, where a ferry at the Lower Lode provided access to the opposite bank. But that would be a slow process, and the only bridge lay beyond it, another six miles away at Upton on Severn.

The Cerne Abbas Giant, above the village and abbey of Cerne, along the road taken by the Lancastrians on their march from Beaulieu. Queen Margaret was joined here on 15 April by the Duke of Somerset and John Courtenay.

The 15th-century market cross in Malmesbury, the town reached by Edward's army on 29 April.

Things were starting to become uncomfortable again. They were still not across the river, the enemy was now closer thanks to the delay at Gloucester and, to make matters worse, Sir Richard had organised a sortie from Gloucester after the Lancastrians had passed, and seized some of their artillery as it bumped along. At about 4.00pm, the Lancastrians arrived at Tewkesbury at the end of a day's march of 24 miles, footsore and weary.

One mile north of Tewkesbury, in the angle between the Severn and the Avon, was a 1,000-yard ridge known as the Mythe eminence. This was suggested as a strong defensive position as early as 1793 but, as Burne pointed out, if the Lancastrians deployed here they surrendered control of the ferry over the Severn. The ferry could be used either by the enemy to retreat or by Pembroke's reinforcements if they arrived. In any case there was little chance the weary troops could be got across the river before nightfall, and it was probably considered better to make a stand south of the abbey the following morning. It is not known exactly where the camp was situated, though a couple of traditions survive. On the north side of the track joining the Gloucester Road with the Cheltenham Road stood a half timbered building constructed in 1438, Gupshill Manor; a tradition grew up that this is where the Queen rested the night before the battle. Beyond the manor there is an earthwork with five sides each roughly 100ft long, now known as Queen Margaret's Camp, but it is hardly of a size to accommodate an army. It is possible that it is the remains of a grave pit dug after the battle, or as a later memorial.

Meanwhile Edward had brought his own troops along the Portway. The sun rose in the sky and the heat beat down on the men as they marched. The route was along the high ground and was dry and dusty, with little available water. When they arrived in the vicinity of Stroud they crossed the River Frome. The water here, though no doubt a blessing for those at the head of the column, was soon churned up by the wheels of the carts and guns as to be almost undrinkable, says the

THE LANCASTRIANS REBUFFED AT GLOUCESTER
(pages 54–55)

Queen Margaret appeared with her army before Gloucester on 3 May at perhaps 10.00am. Here a herald returns with the news that Sir Richard Beauchamp, warned by Edward's riders, has refused to open the gates (1). We have shown the herald (2) wearing the royal lions and fleurs-de-lys of Henry VI but differenced with a label for Prince Edward as the eldest son. The herald wears long leather riding boots and carries a bonnet. The rider behind carries the Prince's pennon with the Lancastrian swan and feathers (3). Edward, seen at extreme left (4), wears a short gown over his armour, which is visible on his forearms protruding through openings in the sleeves and in the upstanding mail collar. His banner flutters above him, while to its right is seen the Lancastrian royal standard (5) bearing a heraldic antelope. The Queen (6) rides side-saddle, wearing fashionable dress of the day. To her left sits

Edmund, Duke of Somerset (7), who, of royal blood, also incorporates the royal arms but with a border compony in the tabard he wears over his armour and on his banner. Next to his banner is his standard (8) with the silver and gold yale as its main charge. The foot figure in the centre wears Somerset's livery and the portcullis badge of Beaufort (9). The man holding the Queen's horse is also dressed in white and blue livery, which was likewise used by royal retainers (10). The soldier on the far left (11) has a quilted jack but also sports plate leg defences and gauntlets. He carries a glaive, a staff weapon with a long convex blade. He wears the red and black livery of the Prince of Wales with the ostrich feather badge. To the right of Somerset's banner is the banner of Sir John Delves (12), who was destined to be executed after the battle of Tewkesbury. To the right of this is the boar standard of John Courtenay, Earl of Devon (13), and to the right once more the banner of Lord Wenlock (14). (Graham Turner)

author of the *Arrivall*, probably travelling further back in the column. The surrounding area had also been stripped bare of food and fodder. This was presumably the work of local inhabitants, either sympathetic to the Lancastrians, or concerned to prevent it being looted by either of the armies. As it happened, Edward had brought provisions with him, but as yet the men only had a small amount of drink. The army left the Portway on reaching Prinknash, and continued to march via Birdlip, completing the 31 miles from Sodbury to Cheltenham by about 5.00pm. At last they stopped and food was distributed. There was little hope of confronting the Lancastrians that day. By the time they reached Tewkesbury, five miles away, it would be dark and in any case the men were tired and probably still hungry. Edward did not, however, plan to allow Margaret to evade him any longer. He must have intended to attack the following morning and force the Lancastrians to turn and fight. His troops were weary, but then so must be their enemies. Therefore after a short halt he ordered his men to their feet and they moved out of Cheltenham to come within easy striking distance of the Lancastrians the next morning. On arriving in the vicinity of the village of Tredington, Edward ordered the camp be pitched, and the Yorkist army sank thankfully to its rest. The remains of a house traditionally (but with no real evidence) said to be where Edward stayed still exist. Burne worked out that each army had marched 59 miles since 1 May, though the *Arrivall* has 'thirty-six long miles' for the Lancastrians and 'thirty miles and more' for the Yorkists. However, as Burne points out, the eight miles between Cheltenham and Tewkesbury is said in the chronicle to be five miles.

THE BATTLE OF TEWKESBURY

The Battlefield

The area chosen for the battle was bounded on two sides by rivers. To the west the Severn flows from north-east to south-west down towards the Bristol Channel. The River Avon joins the Severn below Tewkesbury from the north-east. The town of Tewkesbury is about 1,000 yards upstream along the Avon, lying on the east bank. There was a watermill on the river and across the main road running through the town lay the abbey. A little west of the abbey a tributary of the Avon flowed past on its southern side, so the town and abbey were bounded on two sides by water. This tributary, the River Swilgate, flowed north past what would become the battlefield, before turning west towards the the abbey. The road from Cheltenham crossed the Swilgate well south of the town and then ran north, on a course more or less parallel to the river, to cross it again at Gander Lane Bridge and enter Tewkesbury. This was the road that Edward would probably use in his advance. Further west, the high road from Gloucester (now replaced by the A38 on a different course that only meets the old road near the outskirts) ran north and also crossed the river near the abbey to pass through the town. Before doing so it crossed Coln Brook, a second tributary of the Avon that flows into it at a point closer to the Severn. South of the town a hillock rises from the ground between Coln Brook and the Gloucester Road. North of the hillock, the Gloucester Road threw off a sidetrack that ran east to join the Cheltenham Road below a rise in the ground. Well to the west of the Gloucester Road the ground sloped up to a wooded park, from whose crest one could look down north-eastwards to the tower of Tewkesbury Abbey. From the other side one looked down to a second, lower road from Gloucester that ran by the river, past the Lower Lode crossing, as

The village of Tredington, some three miles from Tewkesbury, in the vicinity of which Edward made camp on the night of 3 May 1471.

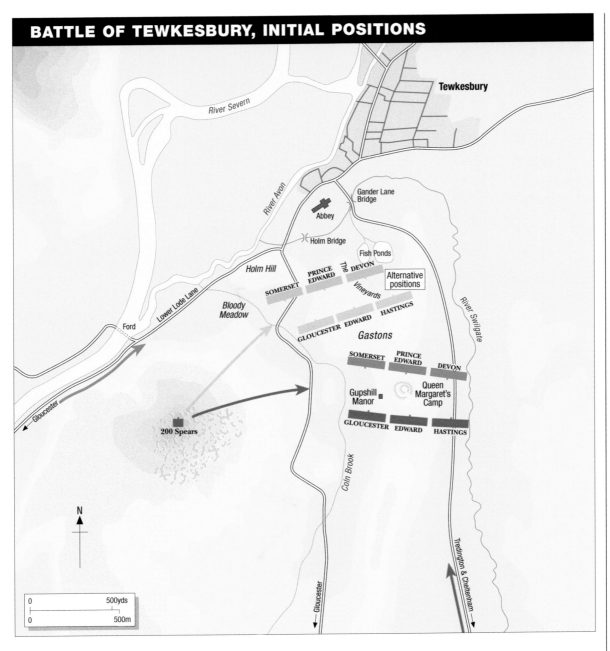

it came into Tewkesbury. It was this road that Queen Margaret had come along. Down the north-east slopes of the hill, where it ran towards the Brook, lay the killing ground that would become known as Bloody Meadow. The ground between the abbey and the east–west track was complicated by the fact that it was very uneven. The *Arrivall* explains:

> *Before them and on every hand foul lanes and deep dykes and many hedges with hills and valleys: a right evil place to approach, as could have been devised.*

Exactly how much of an obstacle these features provided is conjectural today. Certainly there still are many trees that would have obscured the

Aerial view of the battlefield of Tewkesbury, seen from the north. The River Avon flows across the foreground. The River Swilgate runs beyond the housing at upper left, meanders across behind Tewkesbury Abbey, which is on the far lower left, and flows into the Avon at bottom centre. The straight road running parallel to the Avon at right is the low road to Gloucester, along which the Lancastrians probably marched. The main road running down in the centre is the modern A38. Its junction with the road leading off to the right marks the approximate line of the old high road that then crosses Coln Brook (marked by a tree line at extreme right) and turns left. By carrying on in a straight line the road runs up the golf course towards the hill, out of view. Left of Coln Brook lies Bloody Meadow. To the left of the A38 close to the junction is a cemetery that marks the approximate site of the Gastons. The Yorkist centre probably rested somewhere near the distant bend in the A38, and the lines ran across much of the modern housing.

view and broken up movement. Approximately one mile south of the town is a low ridge on which was a large field that was known as the Gastons, bounded on the south by the track that joins the main roads. This southern edge runs approximately 700 yards between the two brooks. From here the ground is flatter before again rising to a second low ridge further south.

Unfortunately for the military historian, large parts of the battlefield and surrounding area have succumbed to modern housing development, which has completely ruined any attempt to obtain an overall impression of the main site. To the east of the A38 modern housing may have destroyed any evidence, and we are forced to turn to old photographs to rediscover the contours of the ground. A second problem is in the location of the battle itself. It is not generally disputed that it took place not far from the abbey, and that the Lancastrians had not crossed the River Avon before being forced to fight. However, there are several possible locations to consider. One of these may be dealt with at the outset, since it was apparent to Burne, writing in the 1950s, that it was flawed. He cites the work of Sir James Ramsey, and while acknowledging the great debt of gratitude owed him for his work on original sources, he points out that already in 1903 Canon Bazeley had commented on errors he had found. Ramsay wrote that Somerset drew up his forces in a line running diagonally north-west to south-east, its left flank resting on the Gastons plateau. Edward approached by the right-hand road and swung left near Queen Margaret's Camp. Here Edward saw the enemy line, being nearly parallel to his line of march. He then arranged his troops and ordered the advance. Gloucester's column

The half-timbered walls of Gupshill Manor. Now a public house by the modern A38, in 1471 it may have stood in the ground between the two armies and probably witnessed the Yorkist army moving forward from the foreground to attack the Lancastrians lined up behind.

was at the head and began the attack. After Somerset's failed diversionary move and the surprise attack on him from Tewkesbury Park, the Lancastrians fled down the slopes towards the Swilgate.

This description was untenable. For one thing, as Burne pointed out, if Somerset's line was in this position, which does not block the road either, he throws away the advantage of ditches and dykes noted in the chronicle, being then 400 yards from them and allowing Edward to form up on drier and higher ground. Moreover, in Ramsay's positioning of Somerset, Edward could simply have charged straight into the left flank and rolled it up, as Somerset himself would attempt during the battle, and as Margaret had done at the Second Battle of St Albans. Ramsay has Gloucester move from left to right to help Edward, when surely Hastings on the right would have done so. The battle is already virtually on top of the hill, which the Lancastrians are said to have been forced up. He sites the park east of the road with no evidence, in contrast to the western site, which was so known in the 15th century, and identifies a wooded lane which hardly fits the description in the *Arrivall*. Ramsay places Somerset on the left (east) of the Lancastrian line when the chronicler states it was the vangaurd (hence on the right), assuming we are looking from the Lancastrian position. Ramsay then says their line was fronted to its rear (the van on the left), with no evidence. If the spearmen's 'hide' was in Margaret's Camp it would not really be an area where fighting took place, yet this is where the only surviving grave pit sites might occur. If the armies lined up as Ramsay suggested, the Lancastrian rout, which is generally agreed to have crossed over Bloody Meadow, would have had to pass the whole Yorkist army.

This leaves two possibilities. The first is that the Lancastrians were drawn up in line not far in advance of the abbey itself. Margaret had obviously reached Tewkesbury with ample time to camp wherever she pleased, and if the camps were close to the fording place at the edge of town to be near the mill, then it would be natural to form up close to the means of escape. However, some would say that this was too close.

A view north across the fields south of Tewkesbury towards the left rear of Edward's line. The road is hidden by trees on the right.

The position left the flanks exposed slightly, since the distance between the River Swilgate and the Coln Brook is much greater than it is further south. Moreover the area becomes a death trap if things start to go wrong, with little room for manoeuvre, with the Swilgate meandering past at the back, and the abbey fishponds a major obstacle if so close to the rear of the lines at the eastern end. One suggestion, made by Colonel J.D. Blyth in 1961, was that a position closer to the town allowed the Lancastrians to make use of the ruins of Holm Castle that crowned Holm Hill and the slopes to the east of it. The old 12th-century castle was burned in 1140 and rebuilt in stone extensively in the 13th century.

Edward leads his men over the obstacles that impede his advance, as he thrusts towards Somerset's men at Tewkesbury. (Painting by Graham Turner)

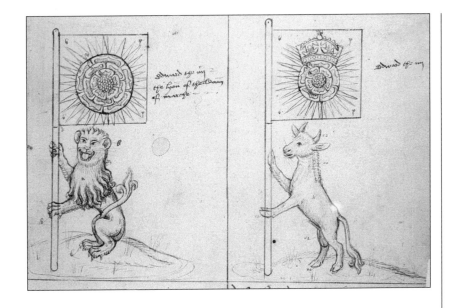

However, as P.W. Hammond has pointed out, there is no evidence from the relative Pipe Rolls, nor in any other document, to substantiate the claim. That there were buildings on the top of the hill, partly in stone and dating from the 13th century, was proved by excavation in 1974–75. Leland commented in about 1540 that the bottoms of some walls could be seen on Holm Hill. As Hammond suggested, this could perhaps also refer to abbey buildings in the low ground around the church, where the word 'holme' (low-lying) might have confused Leland. Whatever was there in 1471, it was hardly enough to deter an enemy or provide a defensible position. Even if the archaeological evidence is taken as meaning there was plenty of stonework on the hill in 1471, or that abbey buildings were substantial at that time, the contemporary narration by

the author of the *Arrivall* simply does not uphold the argument. There
is no mention of Holm Hill as a defended position, let alone a spirited
battle from behind stone walls in any part of the field. If there was one
thing that would have put Edward in a good light it would be an attack
that swept the Lancastrians from solid defences; yet there is nothing.

The second possibility is the one I have adopted here. This places
the Lancastrian line approximately one mile south of the town. Here a
low ridge spreads across east to west, traversed by the modern A38. The
middle of the ridge was at the time laid as field, and known by the name
of 'The Gastons'. From the ridge the ground drops to the south, not a
steep hill but a slope nonetheless. If the Lancastrian line ran along the
southern lip of the ridge, it could rest its left flank by the slope leading
down to the River Swilgate and its right somewhere in the vicinity of the
Coln Brook. This meant that to the south, the ground fell away towards
the trackway connecting the Cheltenham road on the east with the high
Gloucester road to the west. Gupshill Manor would find itself right in
the path of the oncoming Yorkists. Also, if the earthworks known as
Queen Margaret's Camp were in existence in 1471 they would form a
further slight obstacle. It may be that the *Arrivall* partly remembered
descriptions of these when speaking of deep dykes and hills. It also gave
access to the crossing place at Lower Lode, which would have been more
difficult to reach had the army been set further back, when the Yorkists
would have been able to command the approach to it more easily.

The view from the abbey tower across the River Swilgate and over the fields to the left, towards the rear of the Lancastrian line.

THE YORKIST ADVANCE

At first light on Saturday, 4 May, the Yorkist army was stirring. Edward knew he was within striking distance of the enemy and would have every desire to catch Margaret before she could slip across the river with her forces and escape northwards. The king was dressed in his armour, the camp at Tredington was struck and the soldiers prepared themselves, donning their armour and moving into their divisions under their respective lords. As on the march, the Yorkist army formed up into its three battles. The van was led by Richard of Gloucester, behind was the mainward under Edward himself with his brother Clarence near enough to keep an eye on; the rear was led by William, Lord Hastings, with the Marquess of Dorset. Once in order, the banners were unfurled and trumpets sounded. Edward

The rear of the Lancastrian line probably stood on the ridges south of the Abbey, which is out of sight to the right. This view of the ridges is from the western side of the River Swilgate.

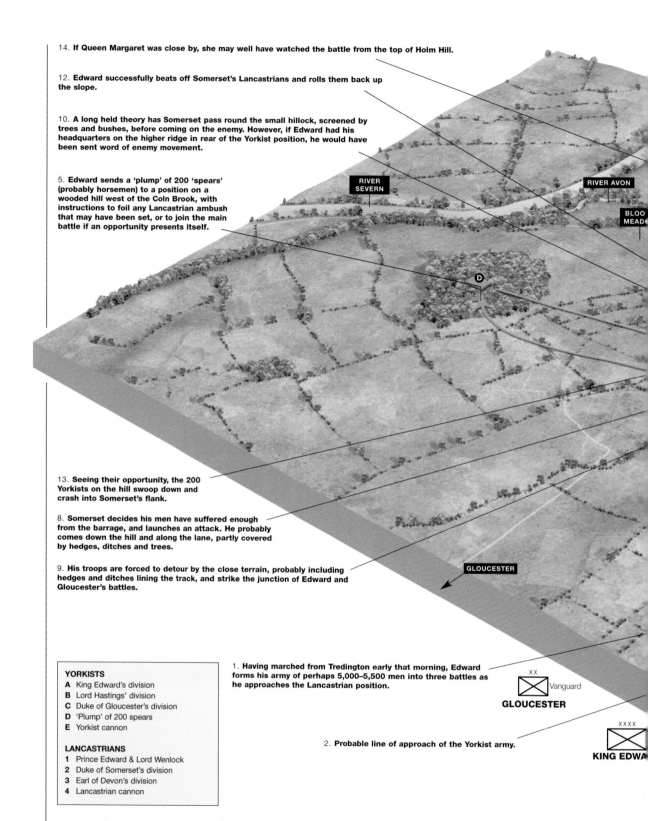

14. If Queen Margaret was close by, she may well have watched the battle from the top of Holm Hill.

12. Edward successfully beats off Somerset's Lancastrians and rolls them back up the slope.

10. A long held theory has Somerset pass round the small hillock, screened by trees and bushes, before coming on the enemy. However, if Edward had his headquarters on the higher ridge in rear of the Yorkist position, he would have been sent word of enemy movement.

5. Edward sends a 'plump' of 200 'spears' (probably horsemen) to a position on a wooded hill west of the Coln Brook, with instructions to foil any Lancastrian ambush that may have been set, or to join the main battle if an opportunity presents itself.

RIVER SEVERN

RIVER AVON

BLOO MEAD

D

13. Seeing their opportunity, the 200 Yorkists on the hill swoop down and crash into Somerset's flank.

8. Somerset decides his men have suffered enough from the barrage, and launches an attack. He probably comes down the hill and along the lane, partly covered by hedges, ditches and trees.

9. His troops are forced to detour by the close terrain, probably including hedges and ditches lining the track, and strike the junction of Edward and Gloucester's battles.

GLOUCESTER

YORKISTS
A King Edward's division
B Lord Hastings' division
C Duke of Gloucester's division
D 'Plump' of 200 spears
E Yorkist cannon

LANCASTRIANS
1 Prince Edward & Lord Wenlock
2 Duke of Somerset's division
3 Earl of Devon's division
4 Lancastrian cannon

1. Having marched from Tredington early that morning, Edward forms his army of perhaps 5,000–5,500 men into three battles as he approaches the Lancastrian position.

X X
Vanguard
GLOUCESTER

2. Probable line of approach of the Yorkist army.

X X X X

KING EDWA

THE BATTLE OF TEWKESBURY
4 May 1471, 8.00–9.00am, viewed from the south-east, showing the Duke of Somerset's assault on the Yorkist line and the Yorkist ambush by the 'Plump' of 200 spears.

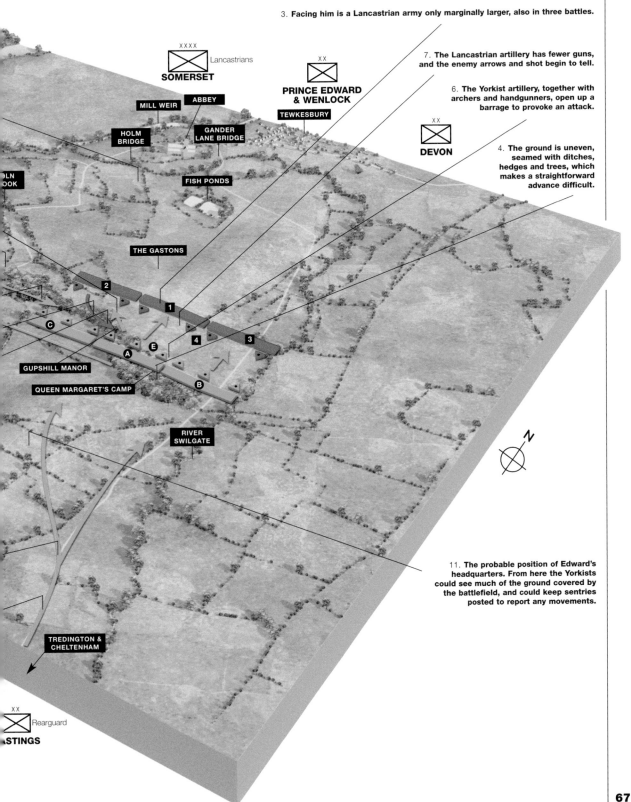

3. Facing him is a Lancastrian army only marginally larger, also in three battles.

XXXX
Lancastrians
SOMERSET

XX
PRINCE EDWARD & WENLOCK
TEWKESBURY

XX
DEVON

7. The Lancastrian artillery has fewer guns, and the enemy arrows and shot begin to tell.

6. The Yorkist artillery, together with archers and handgunners, open up a barrage to provoke an attack.

4. The ground is uneven, seamed with ditches, hedges and trees, which makes a straightforward advance difficult.

MILL WEIR
ABBEY
HOLM BRIDGE
GANDER LANE BRIDGE
FISH PONDS
THE GASTONS
GUPSHILL MANOR
QUEEN MARGARET'S CAMP
RIVER SWILGATE

OLN
OOK

2

C

A
E
1
4
3
B

11. The probable position of Edward's headquarters. From here the Yorkists could see much of the ground covered by the battlefield, and could keep sentries posted to report any movements.

TREDINGTON & CHELTENHAM

XX
Rearguard
STINGS

67

The road up to the slopes of the hill that once may have hidden the Yorkist ambush party. It is now a golf course.

The view from the top of the hill, looking down towards the town and battlefield. The abbey is visible in the left distance.

'committed his cause and quarrel to Almighty God, to our most blessed lady his mother, Virgin Mary, the glorious martyr Saint George and all the saints'. Then the army moved off, marching north-westwards in good order towards Tewkesbury.

The Yorkist army probably crossed the River Swilgate at Tredington Bridge, though it cannot be proved where the exact crossing point lay, then moving on to the Cheltenham road as it curved up towards Tewkesbury. No doubt his fore-riders kept Edward advised as to the whereabouts of the enemy. As they approached Tewkesbury, the divisions gently climbed until they reached the vicinity of the present Stonehouse Farm, an earlier version of which may have been there in one form or another. This marks the highest point of the surrounding area, and here no doubt the commanders surveyed the ground ahead of them. Edward would have ridden forward at this point, if indeed he had not ridden at the head of his army from the start of the march. Before him the ground sloped gradually down before rising towards the shallow ridge and the Gastons behind. Along that ridge now stretched the army commanded by the Duke of Somerset, as it too was marshalled into position. There is no record of how deep either army was, nor of their exact location. Somerset had positioned himself on the right of the Lancastrian line. The youthful

The Battle of Tewkesbury, as imagined by the Flemish artist who illustrated *The Arrivall of Edward IV* in the late 15th century. (Universiteit Bibliotheek, Ghent, MS 264)

Bloody Meadow, from the side of the road running up the hill. Beyond the trees in the distance lies the Avon.

Prince Edward, last surviving hope of the direct royal line of the House of Lancaster, held the centre; he was accompanied by Lord Wenlock and by Sir John Langstrother, Prior of the Order of St John (the Knights Hospitaller). The left was under the Earl of Devon.

Edward probably ordered his army to form into line at about this point, still well out of bowshot and with room to manoeuvre. He would have seen the heraldic banners proclaiming the position of the Duke of Somerset. Mindful of his reputation, and of the collapse of Hastings' division at Barnet, he decided not to risk setting the latter against Somerset. Instead, he asked his brother, Gloucester, to move left and thus oppose Somerset, rather than lead his men down to the right, the usual place of honour for the vanguard. There is no record of whether Richard felt annoyed at not holding the place of honour, or whether he realised the wisdom of his brother's request and obeyed with a good grace. Nor do we hear if Hastings felt slighted that he was obviously not thought capable of standing up to Somerset. Perhaps Edward, with his usual charm, covered it up by suggesting that Hastings would be in the place of honour. Thus the Yorkist positions at Barnet were used again, but the wings now reversed. It would prove a wise decision.

There is no record of whether either side kept any mounted contingents with the divisions, or whether prickers were roving at the rear to block any desertions and be ready to ride down fleeing enemy soldiers. Hall says before the Yorkists drew too close, Queen Margaret

and Prince Edward rode about the field encouraging their soldiers, promising rich rewards and promotions to those who fought valiantly, a share in the booty that would be seized from the enemy, and especially fame and renown throughout the realm. This last, of course, would appeal to those of gentle birth, who still entertained notions of honour and good name, despite the broken promises, treachery and brutality of the Wars of the Roses. It was the usual pep talk before a hard battle. This may have been more necessary than usual. Hall notes that Margaret had been keen to get the army across the river the previous day and head towards Wales, anxious to meet up with the forces of Jasper Tudor, Earl of Pembroke. It was a view shared by several other captains, who presumably were wary of Edward's reputation, especially after Barnet. Somerset would have none of it, however. He was resolved to settle the matter once and for all, 'to see the final end of his good or ill chance'. Perhaps he was shrewd enough to realise that the tired Lancastrian army would be in a dangerous position if caught as it crossed the river.

After her revue of the troops, Margaret retired and would thence take no part in the proceedings. She may have moved up Holm Hill, where she could have watched the unfolding drama, and would be conveniently in the rear if things went wrong. An unsubstantiated tradition has her watch the battle from the tower of Tewkesbury Abbey. W. Bazeley, writing in 1903, seems to think the Queen spent the battle at Paynes Place, across the River Severn between Tewkesbury and Bushley, but this tradition has no evidence to support it.

The low road from Gloucester, the probable route of Margaret's army, leads into Tewkesbury town, with the Avon to its left. Bloody Meadow lies beyond the right of the picture.

The old mill, where many Lancastrians drowned trying to cross during the rout.

As the Yorkist army was marshalled into line, Edward may have now decided to formulate a ruse that came of past experience. At the battle of Towton ten years earlier, Somerset is said to have placed a squadron in woods on the flank, in the hope of launching a surprise attack on the Yorkists. As events transpired, Edward does not seem to have moved forward far enough to allow this mounted ambush to strike his flank and rear, though they may well have been used to good effect when his troops were hard-pressed. There is also evidence that Edward used the same idea against the Lancastrians at Tewkesbury, partly to prevent Somerset trying it again. Thus the *Arrivall* describes Edward's thinking:

The weir close by the mill.

he considered that upon the right hand of their field there was a park, and therein much wood, and he, thinking to purvey a remedy in case his said enemies had laid any 'bushment [ambush] in that wood of horsemen, he chose out of his fellowship two hundred spears, and set them in a plump, together, near a quarter of a mile from the field, giving them charge to have a good eye upon that corner of the wood, if case that any need were, [and] to put them in devoir [service] and, if they saw none such, as they thought most behoveful for time and space, to employ themselves in the best wise as they could.

Tewkesbury Abbey, the Norman church building in which many took refuge after the battle.

In other words, Edward half expected Somerset to pull off a dirty trick and tried to counter it with a mobile force of 200 'spears', perhaps taken from his reserve. The term 'spears' could mean either cavalry or infantry, but logic insists that here it must mean horsemen; only they could move fast enough to cover a quarter of a mile at the speed necessary to counter enemy action. Edward was giving their commander completely free rein, to use his initiative. We are not told his name but, as events would show, Edward chose well. The exact location of the Yorkist 'plump' (which seems to mean a mass of men) is likely to have been up the slope of the hill to the west of the battlefield. From this hill a commanding view of the area below is afforded. It also happens to command the Lower Lode crossing down the slope to the north, which could have been seized

The sacristy door inside the abbey, its inner side covered with plates said to be from coats of plates worn by soldiers at the battle. Since the coat of plates had by this date given way to the brigandine, which was lined with smaller plates, this story has to be treated with care.

by mounted men galloping downhill to block escape. In the event, their services were to be used elsewhere.

The Yorkist line now moved slowly towards the waiting enemy. If the divisional archers had been mounted for the march that morning, they would now be on foot as they approached their targets. In front lay the track that joined the two roads into Tewkesbury, while the half timbering of Gupshill Manor stood out from the green of the countryside. Perhaps some 5,500 men now moved slowly over the rough ground and down the slope, towards an enemy that was probably slightly larger in numbers. The field might have reminded some of those present of that at Barnet, with thick hedges to obstruct their progress. Hedges may have run along the track that crossed their path. However, whether the author of the *Arrivall* overemphasised the size and quality of these obstructions, to highlight the achievements of his king, is debatable. It cannot have been easy for those in full plate armour to cross the rough ground. Any wearing Italian armour would have great difficulty in seeing the ground immediately at their feet through the visors of their *armets*, since neither the visor nor the lower faceplates were provided with the breathing holes that aided vision.

Nonetheless, the Yorkists came on without losing their order to any degree. Edward had brought some field guns, which had also been hauled over the grass. As they closed to extreme bowshot, some 300 yards, the guns were slewed into position. Edward, it seems, probably realised that Somerset was weaker in ordnance, since he had been denied entry to Gloucester and had lost part of his artillery to its commander. He therefore decided on a pounding match, supported by his archers and, though not mentioned, handgunners. The guns roared and the archers loosed off 'right-a-sharpe shower'. Since the *Arrivall* speaks of the 'King's ordnance', it may imply that most of the guns were in the centre, but Gloucester may also have had royal ordnance, of course. The *Arrivall* mentions the van as being in action with their archers, which may suggest that those under Gloucester in the van were the first to start firing. Perhaps they had the best shot at the target; certainly we are told that the King's ordnance 'was so conveniently laid before them'. The Lancastrians returned the fire, but because 'they had not so great plenty', as the *Arrivall* notes (though not specifying whether the shortage was only of artillery or both shot and arrows), they were obviously getting the worst of the duel. It is possible that the guns not only fired stone balls but a primitive form of canister, made from stones and other sharp objects, since it had been known as an anti-personnel weapon since about 1400, at least in Germany. Certainly the effects of the cannon and the arrows began to tell, and the Duke of Somerset began to calculate how to counter this situation and perhaps win the battle.

SOMERSET'S GAMBLE

What follows is perhaps the most controversial part of the battle. The author of the *Arrivall* is not sure what prompted the Duke of Somerset's next move, whether it was the fact that his men could not take the punishment from the bombardment, or whether he simply wanted to make a courageous move. As it says, Somerset:

SOMERSET'S ADVANCE AT TEWKESBURY (pages 74–75)
Edmund, Duke of Somerset, launches his attack on the
Yorkists, passing over the track lined by hedges, trees and
ditches as his men come to grips with the Yorkists. The
attack may have been prompted by the desire to silence the
Yorkist guns and to beat back their archers, who seem to
have outnumbered the Lancastrians. Somerset himself is
marked by his square banner with the royal arms with a
border compony (1). His long-tailed standards, rallying point
for his troops, wave above his men (2). Two billmen advance
in the centre, their coats bearing Somerset's livery and
portcullis badge (3). Marching to meet the Lancastrians is
the Yorkist centre division, whose standards bear the sun in
splendour and the lion (4). In the foreground a struggle
ensues to capture one of the culverins (5). This was a light
field gun with a pivoting split trail that allowed the barrel to
be elevated, the top half of the trail being held in the
required position by the peg on the perforated upright at
the rear. It was a breech-loader; two chambers that hold

charges of powder lie on the grass, one being easily
changed for another after discharge. Each chamber was
secured in position in the breech by the chained wooden
wedge, using the hammer lying close by. The sponge for
swabbing out smouldering debris after each shot is propped
against the axle. One of Somerset's retainers wrestles with
a Yorkist; the Lancastrian wears an open-faced sallet in
contrast to the others visored variety (6). A knight in west
European plate armour tries to fend off the attack on the
guns; he uses a diamond-section hand-and-a-half thrusting
sword, while a rondel dagger hangs at his belt (7). The fluted
ridges on the armour can be seen. Notice that the back
and inside of his thigh is unprotected, the better to feel
his horse when mounted, when the saddle would offer
protection to this area; fighting on foot, he wears no spurs.
Slightly to his left another knight runs forward with a short
pollaxe (8). On the extreme left a retainer wearing the white
boar badge of Richard of Gloucester comes forward, a
painted kettle hat on his head (9). (Graham Turner)

advanced himself with his fellowship, somewhat asidehand the King's van; and, by certain paths and ways therefore before purveyed, and to the King's party unknown, he departed out of the field, passed a lane, and came into a fair place, or close, even before the King, where he was embattled; and from the hill, that was in one of the closes, he set right fiercely upon the end of the King's battle.

The exact meaning of this has caused much debate. Where did Somerset go to with his troops, enabling him to pop out on Edward like a player in some macabre game of hide and seek? Seeing the area today, despite the large amount of building that has gone on, the ground is uneven but hardly so severely that it contains secret tracks, unless these were rendered hidden by hedges, ditches and trees. It is assumed that there has been no major upheaval in the area since 1471. Therefore one possibility is that the track between the two roads was hedged and ditched, and perhaps had not a few trees dotted about it. The main roads too may have been partly of this nature. It is often assumed that Somerset led his men round the small hill just west of the Coln Brook, which, if set with trees, would at least mask some movement. P.W. Hammond has disputed this, pointing out that it would be very difficult to remove a division from the hill without the Yorkists getting wind of some devious intent in the movement of a large body of men, even if screened by others who were ordered to stay. Hammond also makes the point that anyone watching from the hill near Stonehouse Farm would be able to see what was happening, and act to foil it. Even if we accept that Edward was down with his central division at this time, surely he would have left scouts on the hill to report any odd movements to him, particularly if the area in front was so obscured. Why did somebody not ride down to warn him? Perhaps they did, for nowhere does the *Arrivall* actually say that Edward was caught by surprise; it simply says the paths were unknown to him. Indeed, when the Lancastrians appeared he 'full many set forth even upon them', as if taking it all in his stride. So perhaps the deception was tried but was spotted before the surprise attack could be executed. Hammond has interpreted Somerset's movement as coming down in front of the Yorkists rather than moving round in a flanking movement, perhaps in a direct attack to silence the guns and neutralise the archers. In this scenario the Duke aims at the end of the Yorkist line but in the tangle of lanes, hedges and dykes, runs too far east and emerges against the end of the King's battle. This would perhaps be the result of passing across the transverse east–west track, hedged and ditched, or some other obstacle, and then flooding out at the junction of the divisions of Gloucester and Edward. This may have happened; there is no reference in the *Arrivall* to Somerset's destination, it simply states that he passed 'asidehand the King's van'. It seems in fact that he actually wanted to attack Edward, since there is no mention of any mistake in where he ends up; he gets on with the job and starts fighting fiercely. However the text is interpreted, there is a similar outcome. Edward resisted strongly. The retainers, no doubt closely packed, held their ground and began to push the Lancastrians back up the slope towards their lines. Richard of Gloucester joined in and helped to block any progress by the Lancastrians. Holinshed adds that some said it was Gloucester that had pushed back Somerset's attack. We are not told what was happening on

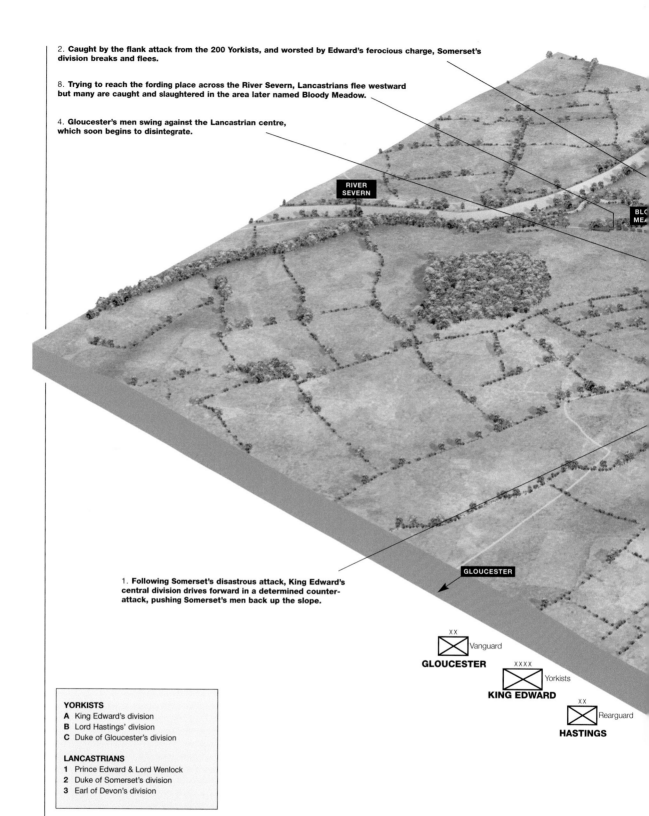

2. Caught by the flank attack from the 200 Yorkists, and worsted by Edward's ferocious charge, Somerset's division breaks and flees.

8. Trying to reach the fording place across the River Severn, Lancastrians flee westward but many are caught and slaughtered in the area later named Bloody Meadow.

4. Gloucester's men swing against the Lancastrian centre, which soon begins to disintegrate.

RIVER
SEVERN

BLO
ME

1. Following Somerset's disastrous attack, King Edward's central division drives forward in a determined counter-attack, pushing Somerset's men back up the slope.

GLOUCESTER

X X
Vanguard
GLOUCESTER

X X X X
Yorkists
KING EDWARD

X X
Rearguard
HASTINGS

YORKISTS
A King Edward's division
B Lord Hastings' division
C Duke of Gloucester's division

LANCASTRIANS
1 Prince Edward & Lord Wenlock
2 Duke of Somerset's division
3 Earl of Devon's division

THE BATTLE OF TEWKESBURY
4 May 1471, 9.00–10.00am, viewed from the south-east showing the aftermath of Somerset's disastrous attack and the collapse of the Lancastrian line.

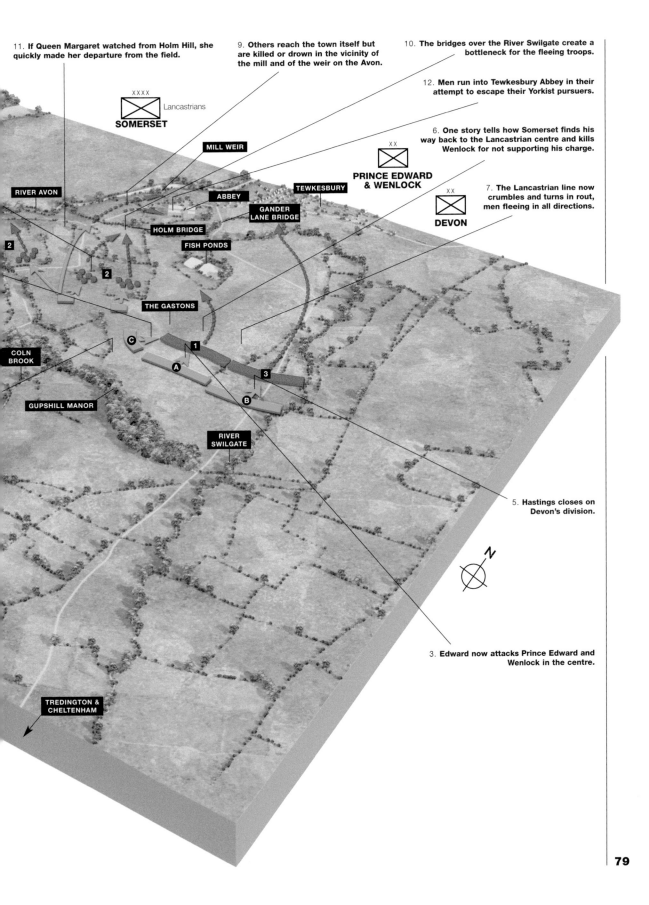

11. If Queen Margaret watched from Holm Hill, she quickly made her departure from the field.

9. Others reach the town itself but are killed or drown in the vicinity of the mill and of the weir on the Avon.

10. The bridges over the River Swilgate create a bottleneck for the fleeing troops.

12. Men run into Tewkesbury Abbey in their attempt to escape their Yorkist pursuers.

6. One story tells how Somerset finds his way back to the Lancastrian centre and kills Wenlock for not supporting his charge.

7. The Lancastrian line now crumbles and turns in rout, men fleeing in all directions.

x x x x
SOMERSET
Lancastrians

x x
PRINCE EDWARD & WENLOCK

x x
DEVON

MILL WEIR

RIVER AVON

ABBEY

TEWKESBURY

GANDER LANE BRIDGE

HOLM BRIDGE

FISH PONDS

2

2

THE GASTONS

COLN BROOK

C

A

1

3

B

GUPSHILL MANOR

RIVER SWILGATE

5. Hastings closes on Devon's division.

N

3. Edward now attacks Prince Edward and Wenlock in the centre.

TREDINGTON & CHELTENHAM

79

the eastern end of the line. The *Arrivall* makes no mention of any specific conflict between Hastings and Devon, and we must presume that only Somerset had at this time come to grips.

Holinshed and Hall give a somewhat different account. At the start of the battle Somerset is within entrenchments, which might be taken for those mentioned by Leland, either the remains of Holm Castle or old abbey buildings. However, Holinshed mentions it being fenced, while Hall states that the Duke had 'trenched his camp round about of such an attitude, and so strongly, that his enemies by no means facile, could make any entry'. This presumably refers to the camp set up the previous night. When battle begins Holinshed maintains that it was not possible to come to hand-to-hand fighting because of all the obstacles. Hall, however, notes firstly an attack by Gloucester's division (with guns, bows or hand weapons is not specified), though his battle 'assaulted the trench of the Queen's camp, whom the Duke of Somerset with no less courage defended'. It might appear at first glance that here we have the trenches that cause so much trouble, and that the obvious choice is Queen Margaret's camp. Firstly, however, there is no proof of date for the camp. Secondly, as has been noted it is hardly large enough for a substantial force. Also, this earthwork is not on the ridge and would prove hard to defend, given that only a handful of men could actually use it. Therefore we are left with another dilemma. If Somerset was defending his camp from Gloucester, he was hardly using it as a secret route to the main Yorkist army, since it must have been up on the ridge. According to Holinshed and Hall, Gloucester could make no headway and recoiled back, of which debacle Somerset took full advantage to come out of his trench and launch a counterattack with all his division. He expects Prince Edward and Lord Wenlock to follow and back him up, but they do not, whereupon Gloucester turns on seeing the uncertainty transfixing his enemies, and beats them back, entering the trench, with Edward following. Such are the Tudor versions, though here we must remember that their views were Lancastrian and not Yorkist, and Somerset is shown bravely coming out to attack, not using a hidden route to launch a surprise. It is intimated that he has the smaller division, and loses because he is let down by the mainward not backing him up.

Whatever actually happened, things did not go at all according to Somerset's hopes. He may have come down against Gloucester to silence the Yorkist guns and force the archers to pull back, and if it was a straightforward frontal attack rather than a clever flank move his men may simply have come up against a thick hedge perhaps along the track, or some other obstacle, channelling them further east until they could come to grips with the enemy. It may be that Somerset wanted to strike at Edward's division to bring the battle to a climax quickly, to settle things one way or the other, as Hall had intimated. Either way, he struck the end – presumably the western end – of the mainward. This sounds worse for Edward than it probably was. We are used to seeing divisions neatly laid out on maps with a sizeable gap between each one for clarity. In practice this would hardly be noticeable. For one thing each division contained men fighting for various lords, and each group wearing his livery. The overall command might be given to a magnate, prince or king, but men knew whom they fought for as divisional head and were unlikely to think neighbours wearing different liveries in the next

St Mary's Church, Luton, commemorates Lord Wenlock. Two helmets have been tentatively associated with him. One has a hole in the skull but is of 17th-century date. The other is made up of pieces of various dates but does have a visor from an *armet*, though on balance this too is more likely from the early years of the 16th century than the time of Tewkesbury.

division were part of their own. Thus there would be no problem in closing the three divisions in practice into one solid line, to prevent any penetration by the enemy, just as men were taught to keep close for the same reason. Equally, the *Arrivall* does not state that Somerset was aiming at the corner of Edward's division. Probably the lines collided as they skirted the obstacles between them.

Whether or not the Tudor accounts are based on sound evidence – and they differ somewhat from that of the *Arrivall*, whose author was with the army – the failure of the Lancastrian centre to support Somerset's van is highly plausible. This would account for the success of the Yorkist centre in pushing back his men towards the rest of their lines, assisted by the van under Gloucester. At the same time, the commander of the plump of spears on the hill added to the discomfort of the Lancastrian van. Seeing no sign of any threat to the Yorkist army from the woods, he realised he was now free to use his men as he saw fit; now his chance had come, and he used it to full effect. The 200 spears came down the slope of the hill and across the road and Coln Brook, to charge into the flank and rear of Somerset's men. This was the final straw. Realising they were outnumbered and unsupported, shaken by this unexpected onslaught, they gave ground and started to break up.

Holinshed and Hall tell an extraordinary tale of how Somerset reacted to the lack of support from his divisional commander. Coming up to where Lord Wenlock was standing immobile, he railed at him and called him a traitor. Then, in a fury, he swung his axe and brained the other with it. The *Arrivall* simply names Wenlock as among the notables slain, without further elaboration.

The battle was effectively over. There was no time for further argument, as the entire Lancastrian line broke up. If the Tudor writers are correct, we do not know why the centre refused to engage. It appears that after the van broke up Edward turned his attention to the Lancastrian centre, but it did not stand for long, for, says the *Arrivall*, after a short while, it was put to flight. There is no record of what happened on the east of the line. Logic would suggest that Hastings moved his men up as Edward advanced, so as not to leave the centre's flank exposed, though whether his men came to grips with the enemy is not stated. The Earl of Devon is mentioned as among those killed, but could have died in the rout.

Now men were running in all directions to escape. The *Arrivall* says that many ran into the park, the meadow that was nearby, and also the lanes and dykes, hoping to escape that way. Some ran back towards the monastic complex, but had to get across the River Swilgate. There would have been congestion around the two bridges, Holm Bridge and Gander Lane Bridge, as men struggled to push across. Some sought refuge in the town, others ran through the streets down to the banks of the Avon by the old mill, where there was a ford. However, many drowned in their eagerness to cross, and others no doubt died as Yorkist prickers came galloping up to the crowds trying to get into the water. Knights and other men-at-arms may have called up their horses from the baggage park to join in the chase, and perhaps even some archers, eager for ransom money or loot. Many Lancastrians streamed away westwards towards the fields beyond the Coln Brook, where lay the road to Gloucester and also the Lower Lode ferry. Yorkists caught up with many of them here and cut them down in the fields, which was given the name of 'Bloody Meadow' (already in 1497 the name 'Blodyfurlong' is recorded, and 'Bataylham' in 1528/29). The *Arrivall* says that Prince Edward was taken while fleeing towards the town, and slain in the field, and all contemporary writers uphold this view. Even Warkworth, with Lancastrian sympathies, describes the Prince as being slain in the field while crying for succour to his brother-in-law, the Duke of Clarence. However, in about 1473 Waurin notes in his *Histoire de Charles, dernier duc de Bourgogne*, that although Edward died in the field, others said he was captured, disarmed and then struck across the face by Edward with a sword, followed by everyone else. The story then grew; the Tudors Hall and Holinshed assert that King Edward offered an annuity of £100 for life to anyone who could bring him the Prince, either alive or dead, and the Prince's life to be saved. Sir Richard Croftes, a wise and valiant knight, mistrusting nothing, then brings his prisoner to Edward, who demands to know why he comes into his kingdom with banner displayed. After the Prince's spirited reply Edward pushes him away or strikes him with his gauntlet, and the wretched youth is then murdered by Gloucester, Dorset and Hastings.

A large number of refugees fled into the welcoming gloom of the abbey, among them the Duke of Somerset, hoping to be safe in this great house of God from the vengeful Yorkists. Certainly they escaped the fate of being cut down in the rout, but there is dispute over what exactly happened in the abbey. With the field finally won and the enemy in flight, Edward approached the abbey to give thanks for his victory. The *Arrivall* would suggest a general pardon:

> he gave them all his free pardon; albeit there neither was, nor had [not] at any time been granted, any franchise to that place for any offenders against their prince having recourse thither; but that it had been lawful to the King to have commanded them to have been drawn out of the church, and had [done] them [to be] executed as his traitors, if so had been his pleasure.

It goes on:

> he granted the corpses of the said Edward, and others so slain in the field, or else where, to be buried there in church, or else where, [as] it pleased the servants, friends, or neighbours, without any quartering, or defouling their bodies, by setting up at any open place.

This is not quite the picture presented by Warkworth, who says Edward entered carrying a sword in his hand and was faced by a priest 'that turned out at his mass, and the sacrament in his hands'. According to this account the priest:

> required him by the virtue of the sacrament, that he should pardon all those whose names here follow: the Duke of Somerset, the Lord of Saint John's, Sir Humphrey Audeley, Sir Gervais of Clifton, Sir William Gremyby, Sir William Cary, Sir Thomas Tresham, Sir William Newburgh, knights; Harry Tresham, Walter Courtenay, John Florey, Lewis Myles, Robert Jackson, James Gower, James Delvis, son and heir to

Sir John Delvis; which, upon trust of the King's pardon, given in the same church, the Saturday, abode there still, when they might have gone, and saved their lives.

In other words, the men in the abbey trusted Edward's promise and stayed where they were instead of trying to slip away while there was a chance.

The *Chronicle of Tewkesbury Abbey* presents a similar story, that Yorkists entered the abbey armed and killed several of those sheltering inside, while others sacked the building and the town. As a result the abbey had to be consecrated again on 30 May by the Bishop of Worcester. Similar violence occurred at the church at Didbrook, some ten miles away, where Lancastrians were rooted out, as noted in an enquiry the following year. It was rebuilt six years later by the Abbot of Hailes Abbey.

AFTERMATH

Edward knighted a number of followers, including George Neville, Phillip Courtenay, Richard and Ralph Hastings, and James Tyrell. Tradition places this at Grafton but since this is several miles away it could be a mistake for 'Gastons', which is more likely. On 6 May the fugitives led from the abbey were brought to trial before Richard of Gloucester and the Duke of Norfolk, as Constable and Marshal of England respectively. Condemned for treason, Somerset, together with Sir John Langstrother, Prior of the Hospitallers, Sir Gervase Clifton and about ten others, were taken to the market place in Tewkesbury and publicly beheaded. It was perhaps the only sensible option open to Edward. Several had already been pardoned once and betrayed the trust Edward had placed in them. There was no way any of them could be let loose to cause further trouble. A number of others, however, were pardoned, such as Sir Henry Roos. It had been a disastrous year for the Lancastrian cause. Barnet had seen the power of the Nevilles snuffed out; now Tewkesbury had removed the last male Beauforts and had seen Prince Edward killed. The pathetic figure of King Henry was secreted securely in the Tower of London. Queen Margaret had fled. Jasper Tudor, Earl of Pembroke, remained, but he was not in the direct line of the House of Lancaster. Nor was Henry Tudor, whose rather weak claim came through his Beaufort mother, and who in any case was in exile in Brittany. It looked like Edward had at last secured the crown of England for the House of York.

However, news came in at once of more trouble. Before 3 May Thomas Neville, Bastard of Fauconberg, had landed in Kent and was busy inciting rebellion. With him were reinforcements of 300 men supplied by Sir Walter Wrottesley and Sir Geoffrey Gate, Lancastrians who commanded Calais, and Richard Whetehill and John Blount, who commanded the nearby castles of Guines and Hammes. Meanwhile in the north trouble was fomenting, as a result of news reaching there of Queen Margaret's landing. Worried that the northern revolt might spread, Edward decided to deal with that first, and on 7 May he marched from Tewkesbury. He hoped that Earl Rivers and the Earls of Essex and Arundel, Sir John Scott and the London authorities could contain Fauconberg. On the way to Worcester he heard that Queen Margaret had been captured. Having fled on seeing her army defeated, she was found in 'a poor religious place', according to the *Arrivall*, where she had retired on the Saturday morning of the battle after her son had gone to take his place on the field. Hammond has pointed out that this seems unlikely to have been the case until the battle was lost, since there was no cause for her to expect they would be defeated. If she then decamped there, it may have been Little Malvern Priory, *en route* for Wales or perhaps Lancashire. Hall, however, says she was captured in her

The death of the Duke of Somerset, as illustrated in *The Arrivall of Edward IV*. Although shown here in open country, he was executed in the market place in Tewkesbury. (Universiteit Bibliotheek, Ghent, MS 264)

The attack on London by the Bastard of Fauconberg, from *The Arrivall of Edward IV*. (Universiteit Bibliotheek, Ghent, MS 264)

carriage, 'almost dead for sorrow'. Warkworth lists those captured with her: Anne Neville, wife of Edward of Lancaster, the Countess of Devon, and Lady Katherine Vaux. All their husbands had died in the fighting. Edward must have been mightily relieved to hear the news, since Margaret was such a thorn in his side that there would be no peace while she was at large to stir up trouble. However, the death of her son, her main hope, had probably broken her spirit at last. Edward arrived at Coventry and waited from 11 to 14 May for more soldiers to augment his own troops, who had already undergone the ordeal of forced marches and battle. Here he was met by the Earl of Northumberland, who brought the news that the northern rebels had melted away on learning of the disaster at Tewkesbury. Leaderless following the deaths of the Nevilles, men had turned to Percy, the only great noble in the area with real power, and he had no intention of confronting Edward. The latter was now free to turn his attention to the south, and it was propitious that he did so.

In contrast to the northern rebels, those in Kent had no intention of backing down on hearing of Edward's victory. Fauconberg had now behind him the men from Calais plus others from the Cinque Ports and gentlemen and yeomen from all over Kent. Some of the unrest may have been caused by a desire for good government but a number of poorer men and criminals, especially in London, saw it as an excuse for looting and plunder. This threat stirred the mayor and council to resist the rebels, something not many towns had done during the Wars of the Roses. Another rising in Essex seems to have been as much about protesting at low prices paid by London buyers for dairy produce. Men from Surrey also joined in. Some men may have been simply bullied into joining. Fauconberg's ships sailed up the Thames towards London and, on 12 May, the rebel forces demanded entry. The defiant citizens refused; the mayor, aldermen and leading lights of London encouraged their men, while overall command seems to have been under the Earl of Essex leading a group of knights, esquires and gentry as a kind of mobile force whose military prowess boosted the morale of the citizens. The Tower contained Earl Rivers, while the constable, Lord Dudley, had 100 soldiers staying there for 21 days from 21 April. Payment was made for 77 bundles of 2 shilling arrows and 99 bundles of 18 pence arrows, plus various small lead pellets. A wall in St Katherine's opposite the Tower was demolished 'for the defence of the said Tower'.

When the rebels pushed forward at London Bridge they were beaten back. On 13 May they made a failed attempt to cross the Thames at Kingston to attack Westminster and the neighbouring suburbs, or they may have intended to march against Edward. Earl Rivers had sent men in barges to strengthen the defence of Kingston. Rivers did speak with Fauconberg on Kingston Bridge, says *Warkworth's Chronicle*, and managed to persuade the rebel leader to return to his ships. Edward was now collecting more troops and was preparing to set out, though he did not actually do so until 16 May, so Fauconberg may have been afraid of being trapped against the walls by the royalist army. Next day saw Fauconberg back with his men in St George's Fields, between Lambeth and Southwark. They tried again to break the will of the city, bombarding it with their cannon. At the same time a second assault was made on London Bridge, and houses on the south bank side were fired. A third assault was by troops

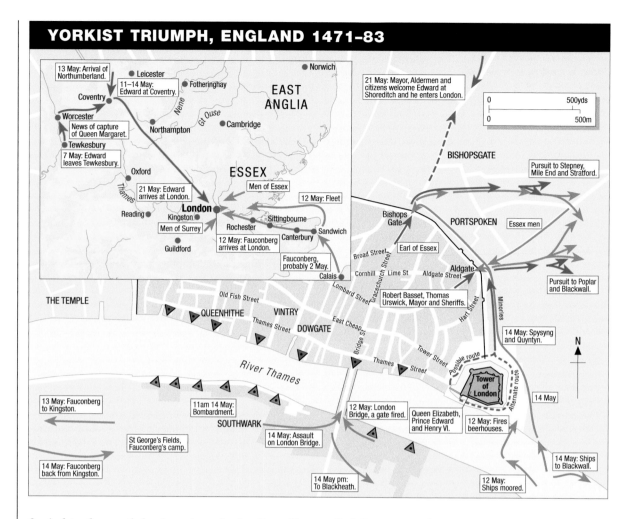

YORKIST TRIUMPH, ENGLAND 1471–83

13 May: Arrival of Northumberland.

11–14 May: Edward at Coventry.

● Leicester

● Norwich

● Fotheringhay

Coventry

Worcester

News of capture of Queen Margaret.

Tewkesbury

7 May: Edward leaves Tewkesbury.

Oxford ●

EAST ANGLIA

● Cambridge

Northampton ●

ESSEX

Men of Essex

21 May: Edward arrives at London.

Reading ●

London

Kingston ●

Men of Surrey

Rochester ●

12 May: Fauconberg arrives at London.

Guildford ●

Sittingbourne ●

Canterbury ●

Sandwich

12 May: Fleet

Fauconberg, probably 2 May.

Calais ●

21 May: Mayor, Aldermen and citizens welcome Edward at Shoreditch and he enters London.

0   500yds

0   500m

BISHOPSGATE

Pursuit to Stepney, Mile End and Stratford.

Bishops Gate

PORTSPOKEN

Essex men

Broad Street

Cornhill   Lime St

Earl of Essex

Aldgate

Aldgate Street

Pursuit to Poplar and Blackwall.

Lombard Street

Gracechurch Street

Robert Basset, Thomas Urswick, Mayor and Sheriffs.

Hart Street

Minories

14 May: Spysyng and Quyntyn.

N

THE TEMPLE

Old Fish Street

QUEENHITHE

VINTRY

Thames Street

DOWGATE

East Cheap

Bridge St

Thames Street

Tower Street

Possible route

Tower of London

Alternate route

14 May

13 May: Fauconberg to Kingston.

River Thames

11am 14 May: Bombardment.

SOUTHWARK

St George's Fields, Fauconberg's camp.

14 May: Fauconberg back from Kingston.

14 May: Assault on London Bridge.

12 May: London Bridge, a gate fired.

Queen Elizabeth, Prince Edward and Henry VI.

12 May: Fires beerhouses.

14 May: Ships to Blackwall.

14 May pm: To Blackheath.

12 May: Ships moored.

ferried to the north bank under a leader from Essex called Spysyng, and also one named Quyntyn, who then marched up to assault Aldgate while another party attacked Bishopsgate. The former were joined by more men from Essex. The attacks were partly co-ordinated though they failed to all begin at the designated time of 11.00am. The City was hard pressed but resisted gamely. The guns on the north bank, meanwhile, gave as good as they got. By hard pounding they eventually broke the will of the gunners on the opposite bank and forced them away. Those mounted at the end of London Bridge were able to sweep rebels off it, despite the latter having burned 13 houses on the bridge. However, the rebels had managed to start fires in three places in the City. They captured the outworks of Aldgate, the citizens retreating under the gate, whose portcullis came down to block the gap, killing several rebels and trapping others in the gate passage, to be slaughtered. Guns fired at the citizens hit more of the stone work and the portcullis than their intended target. Robert Basset, alderman of Aldgate ward, 'wearing a black jack or doublet of fence', together with Thomas Urswick, ordered the portcullis raised. Together with the mayor and sheriffs, and with trumpets blowing, they led a charge against the rebels outside. At the same time Earl Rivers issued from the postern in the Tower, probably that by the Byward Gate, and swung round and up the road to hit the rebels in the side. This double blow was enough; they broke and fled,

Several stone cannonballs have been preserved in the collection of the Royal Armouries at the Tower of London, some having been found in the moat and likely to have been fired at the walls from across the river during the attack by Fauconberg.

back towards Mile End. Chased by vengeful defenders, the pursuit was carried as far as Stratford, some five miles distant. At the same time the Earl of Essex charged out of Bishopsgate and overthrew the opposition there. Sir Ralph Josselyn also chased the rebels back to Blackwall, also five miles from the City, where the ships had been transferred, and many died trying to board them. Josselyn killed many others as his men returned. The *Arrivall* puts the number at 700; modern estimates are perhaps 300. Some of those captured were later ransomed. Men who fought at Mile End and elsewhere later received two barrels of red wine. The rebels on the south bank, and presumably the remnants on the north who would be carried across, now retired to Blackheath, while the fleet sailed that same night, 14 May, and came to Sandwich. Fauconberg left the rebel force on 18 May, travelling with the men of Calais to Sandwich by way of Rochester. His men took ship and he waited for the king, presumably a deal having been struck. The rebels on Blackheath remained a day and night longer, then broke up. On Tuesday, 21 May, the mayor, aldermen and citizens met Edward at Shoreditch outside the City. He knighted the Mayor, John Stokton, Thomas Urswick the Recorder, John Crosby, a sheriff, and nine aldermen. He then entered London with his army, banners unfurled and trumpets and clarions blaring. Richard of Gloucester led the way, while Queen Margaret entered in a cage at the rear. A service of thanksgiving was held at St Paul's. That night, Richard entered the Tower as Constable, and by morning Henry VI was dead. It was almost certainly ordered by Edward himself.

Next morning the body of King Henry was brought on a bier from the Tower to St Paul's, accompanied by torch bearers and armed guards from the Calais garrison. After lying with the face exposed to make sure everyone knew the old king was dead, the new king had the body transferred next day to the Black Friars in London for a generous funeral service, thence by barge down the Thames to Chertsey Abbey where it was laid to rest. Meanwhile Richard of Gloucester was riding into Kent with royal troops, to be followed by Edward with Clarence, Norfolk, Suffolk, Rivers, Hastings and others. Richard made for Sandwich, where Fauconberg had already been parleying via one of Clarence's heralds.

Edward reached Canterbury on 26 May, while Fauconberg was surrendering himself and his 47 remaining ships to Richard. Whilst at Canterbury, Edward supervised an investigation into the revolt, resulting in over 100 persons being named as active rebels and a similar number as offering material assistance. Many were executed, including Nicholas Faunt, the mayor of Canterbury, who was taken to the Tower and then back to Canterbury to be hung, drawn and quartered. Spysyng and Quyntyn were also executed, their heads perhaps fittingly spiked on Aldgate. On 15 July royal commissioners enquired into the revolts in Surrey, Kent and Essex. Canterbury, Sandwich and other Cinq Ports lost their privileges, while heavy fines or executions were inflicted, particularly in Essex, where men were hung along the road from the City to Stratford. As the *Great Chronicle* commented: 'Such as were rich were hanged by the purse, and the other that were needy were hanged by the necks'. That same month Edward received the submission of the garrison in Calais, and pardons were issued for men of note there. Hammes too submitted, and with such pardons he weaned a number of Lancastrian supporters who then proved faithful servants.

Fauconberg for his part accompanied Richard when he went north, but by 11 September his goods had been seized and he was branded a traitor. His change of heart had been very brief and he seems to have raised another revolt, this time with his brother, William, yet another Bastard of Fauconberg. This time he did not escape so lightly. While his brother reached sanctuary at Beverley, Thomas was executed and his head fixed on London Bridge looking towards Kent, a somewhat grisly royal joke.

In October, Edward declared a general pardon. George Neville was released from the Tower, though he was arrested again on 25 April the following year, sent to the Tower and next day shipped to Calais where he stayed until pardoned again in November 1474. Edward rewarded his followers, especially his fellow exiles Gloucester (who received large parts of Warwick's lands) and Lord Hastings. Rivers, also in exile with him, received his reward only later. Others also benefited; the master of the ship the *Antony* received an annuity of £20, and the pilot 100 shillings. Louis de Gruuthuse was richly rewarded for all his help during the exile. Edward was not to be disturbed again by revolt, and England remained relatively peaceful until his death in 1483, probably from a stroke. The succession of his young son, Edward V, the murder of the boy and his brother, and the taking of the throne by Richard of Gloucester, would finally prompt Henry Tudor to make his bid for the throne and sound the death knell for the House of York.

THE BATTLEFIELDS TODAY

Ironically, both the battlefields of Barnet and Tewkesbury incorporate golf courses, which means that the ground has been worked over to create them. Neither field has produced any great evidence in the way of battlefield relics.

Barnet

The battlefield at Barnet is still in open ground some half a mile north of the town itself. The road from Wood Street, the A411, takes a left turn at the church to become the A1000. This then passes shops and houses until it reaches more open ground. Beyond the battlefield the road forks. The left fork off the A1000 is Kitts End Road, and is the original road to St Albans, down which the Lancastrian army marched (the modern St Albans road, the A1081, turns left off the A1000 a little further south, at a busy junction just below Monken Hadley). The right-hand fork is the continuation of the A1000, the Great North Road, and leads to Potters Bar. On the grass between the two roads of the fork so formed stands the 1740 obelisk, backed by trees. To the north, past Kitts End, lies Wrotham Park. By walking up the right-hand fork for some 300 yards, a lane opens off to the right. This leads into fields beyond the residential housing, and by looking to the right (southwards) the western half of the long ridge can be seen, now covered by well-grown trees. Burn mentioned the tower of Monken Hadley Church, but in his day the trees were obviously shorter. To the left of the lane the fields run into the distance, where Deadman's Bottom is situated, on a level with Wrotham Park to its west across the road. Deadman's Bottom has variously been situated to the north, the north-west and the west, depending on which version of the battle is consulted, but the Ordnance Survey map of the area places it to the north. Either way, fugitives from the battle must have poured across the land surrounding the lane in their bid to find shelter and safety.

If you walk back towards Barnet past the obelisk, and take a left turn down the road that leads past a convent, you can see Monken Hadley Church, which is not mentioned by any chronicler of the battle. Whether the church was there or not, it stands in the vicinity of the Lancastrian left wing, along the ridge. Immediately south of this area the A1000 is flanked by Hadley Common, but even here archaeological surveys have failed to find any major evidence for the battle, since the area has presumably been somewhat landscaped during the 19th century.

Close by on the opposite side of the A1000, an access road leads off westward to a golf club. The car park and restaurant stand in the area of Old Fold Manor, and three sides of the wet moat can still be seen close by, now forming part of the golf course. A thick rough hedge and parallel ditches run from the moat on one side, and another on another

The Byward Barbican on the south side of the Tower of London was a postern latterly renovated by Henry VIII. The assault on Fauconberg's flank may have been launched from here, or perhaps from another vanished postern further east, probably where now stands the Middle Drawbridge.

side. We cannot prove these are contemporary with the battle, and archaeological surveys have not shown any evidence of anything but 19th-century occupation. The golf course has altered the ground contours to some extent, but the 18th green near the moat is a good place to view from, while the 3rd hole also provides decent views. It is suggested that the golfers are approached first for permission to wander on their course.

The road back to Barnet has some period houses set back on the common. One such, Pimlico House, has been suggested as standing on the site of the chapel erected by Edward after the battle to commemorate the dead. It is private but can be viewed from the metalled path leading from the A1000.

Barnet Museum located in Wood Street has several cannon balls on display, found in the vicinity of the battle. Unfortunately these have been identified by the National Army Museum as 3-pdr balls almost certainly used in a firing display on Hadley Common in the 19th century; one clearly displays Roman numerals. A ring, identified by the Museum of London as probably of 15th-century date, was found during controlled metal detector sweeps by archaeologists during the making of the Channel 4 series, *Two Men in a Trench*, along with a possible ferrule from the hilt of a dagger. Little else has been discovered in the ground, despite further organised sweeps, though another ring, with a bear and ragged staff on the bezel, is said to have come from the battlefield, and is now in Liverpool City Museum. The golf course construction has, of course, changed a large area of the natural surface. Despite the rural appearance of much of the rest, Barnet battlefield has been affected by man's dabbling to improve nature since 1471.

Tewkesbury

The field of Tewkesbury has suffered badly from residential development, which has been allowed to completely obliterate large areas of the field. Incredibly, even more would have been destroyed had it not been saved by a number of more conscientious individuals who managed to halt

The remains of the postern gate at the southern end of the City wall, on the northern edge of the Tower moat, viewed from outside the City. Access was on the right of the picture, and may have been an alternative sortie route for the Yorkist garrison.

The palace area of the Tower of London, now mainly grass, with the 13th-century circular Wakefield Tower to the right, the traditional site of the death of Henry VI.

Jean de Waurin presents a copy of his *Croniques d'Engleterre* to Edward IV in 1471, perhaps in Bruges. The other figures are tentatively identified as (from the left) Louis de Gruuthuse, Richard of Gloucester, Hastings and Rivers. (By permission of the British Library, Ms Royal 15 EIV, f.14v)

further 'development'. The fate of Tewkesbury battlefield is a sad comment on our sometimes insensitive attitude to our own history.

The main A38 that runs north towards Tewkesbury today is not the original road. The A38 turns right (east) at a roundabout to bypass the housing development that is part of the battlefield area and meanwhile continues north-west into Tewkesbury as the Gloucester Road. The earlier road ran on a roughly parallel course to the left of the modern road. It rejoins the Gloucester Road below the crossing of the River Swilgate in the vicinity of Holme Hospital, running thence into the town. The old road from Cheltenham to Tewkesbury survives as a footpath.

The abbey still stands, and is easily visited. The church tower, where impressive views of the surrounding countryside are available, may be visited with a guide at certain times. The sacristy door has its metal-covered face on the sacristy side and since this is locked the metal strips are not visible, though a photograph hangs on the wall beside it. In the grounds to the south-east the River Swilgate is visible, as are the ridges in the ground south of the abbey itself.

The area of The Gastons and Queen Margaret's Camp is now rather hidden within modern housing estates. However, the half-timbered Gupshill Manor, now a public house, stands beside the modern A38 north of the modern roundabout.

Tewkesbury Park can be visited by turning off the Gloucester Road, where the ground rises as it ascends the hill. This area is now a golf club, the clubhouse and car park at the summit, where good views are afforded down the slopes to the town below, marked by the abbey. On descending, a marker on the grass beside the same road some 100 yards short of the A38 points the way to Bloody Meadow. This runs at right angles to the road, flanked on the right by thick trees and bushes, and offers a battlefield walk. The path runs towards the River Avon, then joins a metalled road. Turning right on to this, the road Margaret advanced down from Gloucester, leads towards the town along the riverbank and across the A38 to the rear of the Lancastrian positions.

The Old Mill and weir can be reached by taking one of the small roads opposite the abbey that lead down to the riverbank walk. Turning left, the mill is a short walk along the bank, and is now a picturesque restaurant.

By taking the A38 south out of Tewkesbury, a westerly turn beyond the roundabout, opposite Stonehouse Farm, leads down a quiet road towards Southwick Park and offers views on the right (north and north-west) across the fields over which the Yorkist left may have formed. According to some, this was also the route taken by the Yorkist spears to assume position in Tewkesbury Park. To the north is also the area of the hillock and the Coln Brook.

FURTHER READING

Barber, Richard, *The Knight and Chivalry* (Longman Group Ltd, London, 1970)

Bellamy, J.G., *Bastard Feudalism and the Law* (Routledge, London, 1989)

Bennet, J., *A History of Tewkesbury* (1830)

Blair, Claude, *European Armour* (B.T. Batsford Ltd, London, 1958)

Blyth, J.D., 'The Battle of Tewkesbury, 1471', *Transactions of the Bristol and Gloucester Archaeological Society*, Vol. 70, 1961

Boardman, Andrew W., *The Medieval Soldier in the Wars of the Roses* (Sutton Publishing Ltd, Stroud, 1998)

Bradbury, J., *The Medieval Archer* (The Boydell Press, Woodbridge, 1985)

Burne, A.H., Battlefields of England (Methuen & Co., London, 1950)

Cass, F.C., 'The Battle of Barnet', *Transactions of the London & Middlesex Archaeological Society*, Vol. VI, Part 1, Jan. 1882

Contamine, Philippe, *War in the Middle Ages* (trans Jones, Michael) (Basil Blackwell Publisher Ltd, Oxford, 1984)

Davis, R.H.C., *The Medieval Warhorse* (Thames & Hudson Ltd, London, 1989)

Edge, David and Paddock, John Miles, *Arms and Armour of the Medieval Knight* (Bison Books Ltd, London, 1988)

Embleton, Gerry, and Howe, John, *The Medieval Soldier* (Windrow & Greene, London, 1994)

Embleton, Gerry, *Medieval Military Costume* (The Crowood Press Ltd, Ramsbury, 2000)

Foss, Michael, *Chivalry* (Michael Joseph Ltd, London, 1975)

Gies, Frances, *The Knight in History* (Robert Hale Ltd, London, 1986)

Gillingham, John, *The Wars of the Roses* (Weidenfeld & Nicolson, London, 1981)

Grafton Green, B., *The Story of the Battle of Barnet, 1471* (1971)

Haigh, P.A., *The Military Campaigns of the Wars of the Roses* (Sutton Publishing Ltd., Stroud, 1995)

Hammond, P.W., Shearring, H.G., and Wheeler, G., 'The Battle of Tewkesbury', *Tewkesbury Festival Committee*, 1971

Hammond, P.W., *The Battles of Barnet and Tewkesbury* (Alan Sutton, Stroud, ppk, 1993)

Hardy, Robert, *Longbow* (Mary Rose Trust, Portsmouth, 1976, 1992)

Honeybourne, M.B., 'The Battle of Barnet, 1471', *Barnet and District Record Society Bulletin,* No. 13, June 1963

Jones, Anthea, *Tewkesbury* (Chichester, 1987)

Keegan, J., *The Face of Battle* (Pimlico, London, 1991)

Keen, Maurice, *Chivalry* (Yale University Press, London, 1984)

Keen, Maurice (ed.), *Medieval Warfare* (Oxford University Press, Oxford, 1999)

Kendal, P.M., *Warwick the Kingmaker* (1957)

Kinross, John, *Walking and Exploring the Battlefields of Britain* (David & Charles, Newton Abbot, 1988)

Lamplough, Edward, 'The Battle of Barnet', *Bygone Hertfordshire*, ed. Andrews, W., 1898

Lander, J.R., *The Wars of the Roses* (Secker & Warburg, London, 1965)

Maldon, H.E., 'Barnet Field', *Home Counties Magazine*, Vol. 3, 1901

Mann, Sir James, *Wallace Collection Catalogues. European Arms and Armour*, 2 vols (The Trustees of the Wallace Collection, London, 1962)

Myers, R.A., *Household of Edward IV* (Manchester University Press, Manchester, 1959)

Nicholas, Sir Harris, *Wardrobe Accounts of Edward IV* (London, 1830)

Norman, A.V.B., Wallace Collection Catalogues. European Arms and Armour Supplement (Trustees of the Wallace Collection, London, 1988)

Oakeshott, R. Ewart, *The Sword in the Age of Chivalry* (Lutterworth Press, London, 1964)

Prestwich, M., *Armies and Warfare in the Middle Ages. The English Experience* (Yale University Press, London, 1996)

Ramsay, James, *Lancaster and York, 1399-1485*, Vol. II (Clarendon Press, London, 1892)

Rogers, N.J., 'The Cult of Prince Edward at Tewkesbury', *Transactions of the Bristol and Gloucester Archaeological Society*, Vol. 101, 1983

Ross, C., *Edward IV* (1974)

Ross, C., *The Wars of the Roses: A Concise History* (Thames & Hudson, London, 1976)

Rushforth, G.M., 'The Burials of Lancastrian Notables in Tewkesbury Abbey after the battle AD 1471', *Transactions of the Bristol and Gloucester Archaeological Society*, Vol. 47, 1925

Seymour, William, *Battles in Britain*, Vol. I (Sidgwick & Jackson Ltd, London, 1975)

Thompson, M.W., *The Decline of the Castle* (Cambridge University Press, Cambridge, 1987)

Turnbull, Stephen, *The Book of the Medieval Knight* (Cassell, London, 1985)

Visser-Fuchs, 'A Ricardian Riddle: the Casualty List of the Battle of Barnet', *The Ricardian*, Vol. 8, 1988

Original Sources

'The Rose of Rouen', *Archaeologia* 29 (1842, pp. 343-7)

Bruce, John (ed.), *Historie of the Arrivall of Edward IV in England* (Camden Society, London, 1838)

Commines, Phillippe de, *Mémoires*, ed. Dupont, E., 3 vols, Société de l'Histoire de France (Paris, 1840-7)

Gairdner, James (ed.), *The Paston Letters, 1422-1509 A.D.*, 3 vols (1872-5)

Giles, J.A. (ed.), 'Hearne's Fragment', *Chronicles of the White Rose of York* (London, 1834)

Hall, Edward, *Chronicle,* ed. Ellis, H. (London, 1809)

Holinshed, Raphael, *Chronicles of England, Scotland and Ireland*, Vol. 3, ed. Ellis, H. (London, 1808)

Hinds, A.B. (ed.), *Calendar of State Papers and Manuscripts in the Archives and Collections of Milan*, Vol. 1 (1385-1618) (London, 1912)

Kingsford, C.L. (ed.), *Chronicles of London*, 1905 (Vitellius A XVI)

Riley, H.T. (ed.), *Croyland Abbey Chronicle* (H.G. Bone, London, 1854)

Standing, Percy Cross (ed.), *Memorials of Old Hertfordshire* (London, 1905)

Vergil, Polydore, *Three Books of Polydore Vergil's 'English History', comprising the Reigns of Henry VI, Edward IV and Richard III, from an Early Translation, preserved among the Manuscripts of the Old Royal Library in the British Museum*, ed. Ellis, H. (Camden Society old series 29, 1844)

Waurin, Jean de, *Anchiennes Croniques d'Engleterre*, ed. Dupont, E., 3 vols, Société de l'Histoire de France (Paris, 1858-63)

Wesel, Gerhard von, 'The Newsletter, 17 April 1471', by John Adair, *Journal of Army Historical Research*, 1968

Worcester, William, *Annales Rerum Anglicarum*, ed. Stevenson, J. (B. White, London, 1864)

INDEX

(References to illustrations are shown in **bold**)